Navy SEAL Dogs

Also by Mike Ritland

Trident K9 Warriors

NAVY SEAL DOGS

MY TALE OF TRAINING CANINES
FOR COMBAT

MIKE RITLAND

ST. MARTIN'S GRIFFIN ✻ NEW YORK

This is a true story, though some names and details have been changed.

www.stmartins.com

Designed by Kelly S. Too

The Library of Congress has cataloged the hardcover edition as follows:

Ritland, Mike.
    Navy seal dogs : my tale of training canines for combat / Mike Ritland.
        p. cm.
    ISBN 978-1-250-04182-1 (hardcover)
    ISBN 978-1-4668-4023-2 (e-book)
    1. Dogs—War use—United States.   2. Ritland, Mike.   3. United States. Navy. SEALs—Biography.   4. Dogs—War use—Iraq.   5. Dogs—War use—Afghanistan.   6. Iraq War, 2003–2011—Dogs.   7. Afghan War, 2001—Dogs. I. Title.
    UH100.R58 2014
    359.9'84—dc23   2013026244

ISBN 978-1-250-04969-8 (trade paperback)

St. Martin's Griffin books may be purchased for educational, business, or promotional use. For information on bulk purchases, please contact the Macmillan Corporate and Premium Sales Department at 1-800-221-7945, extension 5442, or write to special-markets@macmillan.com.

First St. Martin's Griffin Trade Paperback Edition: January 2015

10 9 8 7 6 5 4

This book is dedicated to the brotherhood, and the loyal hounds that help keep them safe.

CONTENTS

Acknowledgments   ix

Author's Note   xi

Map   xii

Prologue   1

PART I: NAVY SEALS AND DOGS

1. A Visit to Chopper and Brett   7

2. A Lifelong Love of Dogs   12

3. A Desire to Serve and Defend   16

4. Combining Passions   20

PART II: ON MAKING THE GRADE

5. Not Your Typical House Pet   29

6. Well Trained   41

7. Prep School for Puppies   51

8. Detection Training: Passing the Sniff Test   60

9. Apprehension Training: Sinking Their Teeth into It   67

10. Distinct Personalities 88
11. The Bond at Both Ends of the Leash 97

PART III: ADVENTURES IN BATTLE

12. Cairo and Lloyd: Among the First 111
13. Samson and Dave: Undeterred Underdogs 122
14. Rex and Dwayne: Foiling Insurgents 138
15. Poncho in Pursuit 151
16. Kwinto's Nighttime Raids 155

PART IV: GIVING BACK AND MOVING FORWARD

17. Carlos and Arko at Ease 163

More About the Warrior Dog Foundation 171
Appendix: A Brief History of Canines in Combat 172
Glossary 185
References 189

ACKNOWLEDGMENTS

I would like to thank the following people, for without them this book would not have been possible.

My parents, George and Sandy—Thank you for putting up with me as a kid and instilling the values and foundation that forged me into the man I am today.

The SEAL Teams—Enlisting at eighteen, I grew up in the teams. There could not have been a finer collection of warriors to be around to set the example of how to live your life. The entire country owes you an infinite debt of gratitude for the violence you bestow on our enemies.

Marc Resnick, his assistant Kate Canfield, and everyone at St. Martin's Press—Thank you for your professionalism and pride in what you do. It's been a pleasure working with you.

Gary Brozek—Thank you for the countless hours of hard work you have put into this project, bringing my words to life in a way that couldn't make me prouder.

Brandon Webb—The brotherhood continues to prove that it takes care of its own, and your friendship and advice are certainly no exception. Thank you for everything, brother.

Wayne Dodge—Brother, there are no words to give ample

thanks for what you have done for me, in more ways than one. Your friendship will be forever appreciated.

The warriors (both men and dogs) at MPC-1 (Multi-Purpose Cammo)—You guys are the reason I do what I do, and I could not be prouder of the job you guys have done and continue to do.

Special thanks to:

The Allon Family	CP
Happy	SA
Fro	Cinnamon Bear
BC	Johnny D
Mike Mike	Mrs. Toad
Wimbo	Mike Suttle
DK	Matt Betts
Shrek	Darryl Richey
Del	Trey Straub
Echy	KNPV
Dusty	

AUTHOR'S NOTE

I'm a very lucky man in lots of ways. A lot of men and women haven't returned from our recent wars. I was able to. Now, I combine two passions of mine—working with dogs and still aiding in the defense of our country.

I love dogs as pets and companions. I admire them as workers and useful "tools," and also know how much they benefit from our training and guidance. I feel sorry for anyone who hasn't experienced the joys of seeing a dog in action doing what nature intended or even just the look in a dog's eyes when you scratch "that" spot for him or her. I appreciate all sides of the dog-human interaction enough that I've chosen to make training military and other working dogs my career, while still sharing my life with dogs as pets.

Multipurpose K-9s have saved countless lives. As a nation, we owe them a tremendous debt of gratitude. By telling the story of some of these dogs, I hope to increase awareness of the vital role that military working dogs play. By sharing some of my own story and the stories of some of the Navy SEAL dog handlers I've come to know, I hope to encourage you to believe in yourself and your own dreams, and to keep working toward your goals, because you never know how far you can go—until one day, you realize you're there, exactly where you want to be.

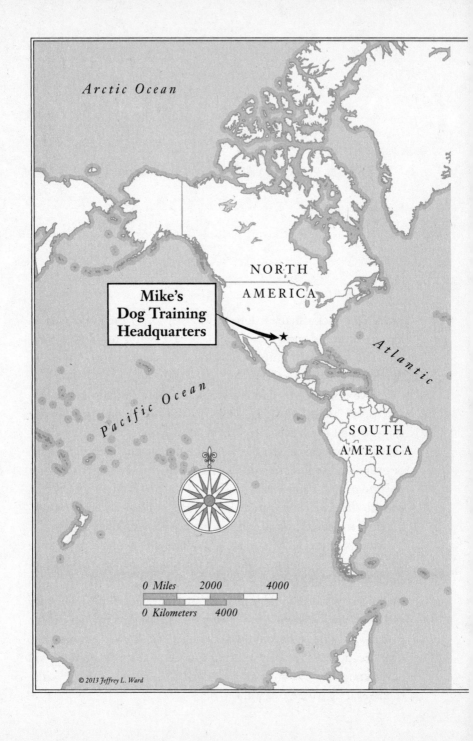

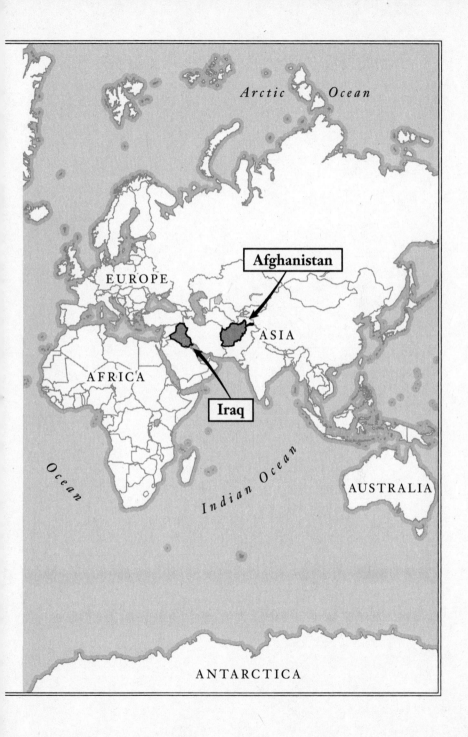

Navy SEAL Dogs

PROLOGUE

The tense silence inside the airborne MH-60 Seahawk helicopter was broken only by the sound of the aircraft's rotors and blades beating like a quickened pulse. Inside, sixteen members of a West Coast–based U.S. Navy SEAL team waited to reach the site of their mission in Northeast Afghanistan. The team was based at a forward operating base (FOB) in Afghanistan, close to the Pakistan border in a mountainous region called the Hindu Kush. In military circles, the Kush is well-known for being an area Taliban terrorists use to travel undetected across the border that divides Pakistan and Afghanistan.

Just a few hours earlier, in a premission briefing, the team had learned the nature of their mission. The operations order commanded them to take out a "high-value target" deemed essential to the Taliban. The target was located in a village about 30 miles (50 kilometers) away. According to the intelligence report, the target was a leading Taliban munitions expert and one of the head trainers who instructed terrorist cell leaders and their underlings in the deadly craft of making improvised explosive devices (IEDs).

As the MH-60 neared the landing zone, everyone on the team felt a collective sense of heightened anticipation. Everyone, including

Chopper, the canine member of the team. From his seat between the knees of his handler, a SEAL named Brett, Chopper's chest rose and fell at a slightly agitated rate in response to the men's eagerness. The men were about to rappel out of the plane into the pitch-black night and into enemy territory, and Chopper was going with them. They all had a job to do.

The copilot radioed that they were several "klicks" (kilometers), or a few miles, from the landing zone. In their briefing, they had learned that there was no landing zone in range large enough or flat enough to accommodate the three helicopters that were on this mission. So they would have to fast-rope in—literally slide down a rope to the ground.

Brett stood and commanded Chopper to do the same. Then Brett turned his back and waited. The platoon chief stepped forward, squatted in front of Chopper, wrapped his arms around the dog's rear end and chest, and lifted him up. Chopper remained alert but still and remained that way when he was strapped into a harness on Brett's back.

Brett felt a *thwack* on his shoulder, a signal that he and Chopper were safely joined together and good to go. Brett spent the next few minutes making his way to the front of the line. He checked the rigging and stepped out of the MH-60's bay and into the dark night air. The dog on his back remained silent. The only sounds were the wind rushing past Brett's ears and the high-pitched whirring of the rope snaking through the device.

Brett and Chopper touched down, and Brett unhooked the line and waited for another team member to release Chopper. He then grabbed the dog's lead, double-checked the harness, and proceeded to the head of the formation. Behind him, the other men moved out of their defensive perimeter position to follow Brett and Chopper, all of them careful to maintain their spacing discipline.

Chopper's years of training and experience, coupled with his honed instincts that had been held at bay during the flight, were now working full force. Steadily moving at a pace between a lope and a trot, with his broad snout alternately pointed to the ground and lifted above his shoulder to pick up any target odor, Chopper worked along a snakelike path. He was a trained expert at sniffing out explosives and was positioned at the head of the line to detect any IEDs or munitions caches. With his nose guiding him and the platoon, Chopper led the way forward.

After maneuvering for several klicks along a dirt road, Brett noticed a change in Chopper's demeanor. He had anticipated that he'd see a signal from Chopper that indicated the dog had detected the odor of explosives, but Brett was not seeing Chopper's usual body language. Previously, whenever Chopper smelled explosives, he hoisted his tail straight up like a flag and shook it from side to side. It reminded the men of a rattlesnake alerting others to its presence. In addition, his movements became more rapid and intense as he zeroed in on the explosives' exact location.

Now Brett was seeing Chopper do something entirely different. The dog's body had gone rigid, and he had assumed the stance of a show dog in the ring: Chopper's head was raised, and he was staring straight ahead. His front shoulders were at attention and stretched forward, and his rear haunches were also straining forward. Brett could feel all that strain and tension on the leash. Then he heard Chopper emit a low, whiny whimper.

Brett knew immediately what the dog was telling the platoon. They were not alone. The enemy was close by, somewhere out there in the dark night.

Brett called out, "Hey, Chopper," and the dog looked at him briefly before resuming his stance. Brett filled the rest of the men in on what Chopper had detected with his nose. The platoon immediately fell out and assumed an antiambush formation, finding cover behind rocks and trees. Brett waited a moment, then unclipped the lead, held the dog by the halter, and whispered, *"Reviere,"* a command that means "Search!" Brett released him, and Chopper eagerly sprang forward and disappeared into the darkness.

Suddenly Brett and the other men heard a ferocious commotion, a combination of dog snarls and human shouts and agonized screams coming from down a shallow embankment yards ahead of them. The forward members of the team advanced to the embankment, and shortly afterward the others heard a few bursts of gunfire. Then the night was dark and quiet again, until the stillness was broken by a SEAL team member calling, "Target is clear."

Chopper emerged from the embankment breathing a little more heavily but unscathed. His head held high, he trotted back toward Brett. The handler knelt and clipped the dog back into his lead.

"*Braafy!*" Brett used a word that Chopper recognized as praise. He petted the dog and ran his hands along Chopper's flanks. Chopper curled into him and lifted his snout into the air. A few other men passed by, each with some sign of praise or thanks for Chopper. Chopper sat there and took it all in, but for him, it was just another day at the office.

Most of the team then busied themselves with defending the perimeter while a small group checked out the embankment. They discovered that four insurgents had been using the embankment as an "ambush nest"—until Chopper came along and caught them by surprise. He had held them at bay, snarling and biting, until the forward members of the team arrived with their loaded rifles.

There was a Russian PKM machine gun, several AK-47s, and hundreds of rounds of ammunition in the embankment. The team cleared the four dead bodies from the site and detonated the munitions and weapons. It was a good night's work for a hardworking platoon, with an unforgettable assist from a well-trained warrior dog with a lifesaving nose.

PART I

NAVY SEALS AND DOGS

1

A VISIT TO CHOPPER AND BRETT

Southeastern California, 2010

The dog lay in the shade of a palm tree, his head up and his ears at attention. He was scanning the desert scrubland, vigilant, the muscles beneath the heavy fur of his flanks taut and ready. Even from behind him, I could see his tongue lolling out of the side of his mouth, flopping like a pink fish.

"Chopper," the man beside me said.

The dog turned to look at us, his expression keenly alert, his dark eyes intent.

"Heerre."

The dog sprang to his feet and made his way across the dusty yard. Under other circumstances, I might have tensed up at the sight of a 75-pound package of fierce determination approaching. However, I could see a very tiny softening of the muscles around his eyes as he neared us and recognition dawned in them. He knew who I was.

He also knew not to approach me first, even though the two of us had spent the first few months of his life in the United States together. As commanded, he came up to Brett, his former SEAL team handler. He sat down alongside the man he served with on dozens of dangerous missions for six years. Now they were living on a small ranch outside Ranchita, California. Brett and Chopper had ceased being on active military duty only three months earlier, but they both would have chafed at being called "retirees."

Chopper sat, still very much at attention, until Brett told him it was okay. Then Chopper looked at me, and I gave his head a few rubs with the flat of my hand. I ran my hand down his shoulder and along his rib cage. He was still in fine fighting form, but I noticed that he relaxed a bit and leaned into me. I smiled at this sign of affection and appreciation for the attention I was giving him.

I noticed that the fur around Chopper's muzzle and eyes had lightened a bit since I'd last seen him. It was no longer the deep ebony that had glowed like a spit-polished dress boot. The slight unevenness to the side of one of his large ears was still there, though. Some scuffle as a pup in his kennel outside of Tilburg in the Netherlands had left him with an identifying mark. In my mind it was never a flaw. Rather, it was a mark of distinction.

"He's doing good," I said to Brett.

"Always. He's a good ol' boy," said Brett. He pushed his sunglasses up and squinted into the distance. "He likes it here. Looks a little like the sandbox, but there's a lot less action. I thought we'd both miss it, but we don't at all." Brett had spent more than a dozen years as a West Coast SEAL team member, the last of his time as a handler working with Chopper.

Having served my own time as a SEAL team member, I knew exactly what Brett meant. The transition from active duty to civilian life takes time for both servicemen and military working dogs (MWDs). Given my experience as a trainer of both Navy SEAL dogs and their handlers, I also understood quite a lot about the deep bond that the two had formed and would share for the rest of Chopper's life.

My trip to visit Chopper and Brett wasn't just a social call. It was a part of a responsibility I take very seriously. I founded a nonprofit organization, the Warrior Dog Foundation, to make certain that retired MWDs are able to live out the remainder of their lives in a positive environment. Though I knew that Chopper was well cared for, I still wanted to check in on him, just like I do with fellow members of SEAL Team Three, or members of other SEAL teams I've come to know in my new role. Whether you're a canine or a human, if you've been a SEAL team member that means you're a brother, and we are all our brothers' keepers for life.

Visiting Chopper and Brett was a privilege and an honor, and, most importantly, it was a great pleasure to see them still together.

In most ways, Chopper is still more fit and more capable than 90 percent of the dogs in this country. Even so, that isn't good enough for the kind of demands a military dog has to meet downrange in places like Afghanistan. Not only is the work extremely demanding, but also the stakes are so high that anything less than the absolute best is not acceptable. It wasn't a question of heart. Chopper still has the drive and determination, but the inevitable toll of age and years of stress has started to creep in.

I knelt down alongside Chopper and draped my arm around him, "*Braafy,*" I said. It always amazed me that something as simple as that short statement of approval could mean so much to a dog that, over the years, teams like Brett and Chopper had developed such a bond of trust that the dog would willingly and gladly place himself in positions of peril.

A few minutes later, Brett and I sat down on the deck he'd recently built. Chopper resumed his perimeter position in the shade. Brett told me a little bit about the enclosure he had built out of split rail and wire. Then he nodded out past the line of post holes that he'd dug and the piles of dirt like overturned funnels flanking them.

"I'm not sure if I'm keeping the coyotes from getting in or Chopper from getting out," he said. "I'm likely doing those varmints a favor either way. Chopper would give them more than they bargained for, no doubt." Brett's voice still had a mild twang that revealed his Smoky Mountain roots.

Inevitably, our talk turned to war stories and to stories of Brett's work with Chopper. Brett recalled one incident, while he and Chopper were still training together, that forged his bond with the dog.

"That time you took us out on that training exercise doing the house-to-house maneuvers." Brett shook his head and smiled. "He got hold of that target and I thought I was going to have to choke him out to get him to release it."

"They do like to bite," I said flatly, underscoring my understatement. "And Chopper does more than most."

"I remember looking him in the eye," said Brett, "and neither of us was willing to give in. Then it dawned on that dog that *he* was the one who was going to have to give in, and it was on account of *me*, and not because *he* wanted to. Then I knew I had him."

Brett said he believed that was the moment when he and Chopper came to truly understand one another. "I think of it this way," he said. "My daddy raised me to fear and respect him, and I did. But with how you conducted the training, Chopper obeyed me because he got the idea that it was the right thing to do and not because he was afraid of me." Brett paused, then said, "Never in my life would I have thought a dog could communicate so much with just a look and his posture."

"It doesn't always happen," I said, "but when it does, it almost defies explanation."

"Hard work and love," Brett added, summing it up pretty nicely, I thought. "Hey, Bud," he said gently to the dog. Chopper turned to look at Brett, his eyes and ears alert. Brett smiled and said, "Good boy."

━ ━

Brett reached into a wooden planter on the picnic table and pulled out a tennis ball. Then he let out a soft whistle. Chopper stood and assumed the position, his ears tilting forward and pointing heavenward, his expression intent. Brett reared back and fired the tennis ball over the enclosure's fence and into the lot beyond. I watched the ball as it arced and then bounced wildly, and then I followed Brett's gaze from the ball's landing zone to the dog, who no longer sat obscured in shadow but was in the warm glow of the setting sun.

"Okay," Brett said at last.

Like a tightly pulled bow and arrow finally being released, Chopper sprang out across the lot, kicking up dust. At the fence he didn't hesitate but easily bounded over the top rail, looking like a champion horse at a jumping contest. I had to laugh as, in his eagerness, when Chopper stooped to clamp down on the ball his front legs splayed out while his rear ones kept churning, and he nearly tumbled over.

His prize captured, Chopper trotted back, munching on the ball, his mouth twisted into a kind of silly, giddy grin. He hopped the fence again and came onto the deck to show us what he'd managed to capture. He sat at Brett's feet, then lowered himself into a relaxed, paws-crossed lie-down, still working on the tennis ball.

Brett looked at me half embarrassed, half pleased. "That's one thing I let him do now," he said.

I nodded. I knew as well as anyone that, in training, Chopper would have been told to drop the ball fairly quickly at his handler's feet. He wouldn't get the reward of gnawing on it. Brett stroked Chopper's head, working his fingers around the backs of his ears as Chopper cocked his head in pleasure.

Finally, Brett said, *"Los,"* and Chopper released the ball. Brett picked it up and offered it to me. I took one look at the spit-frothed ball and declined.

Laughing, I said to Brett, as he stood to throw another one for Chopper, "Wilson. U.S. Open Hard Court. You've got expensive tastes."

Settling back into his seat after letting Chopper go bounding off, Brett grinned with satisfaction and said, "Nothing but the best for my boy. He deserves it."

I couldn't agree more.

2

A LIFELONG LOVE OF DOGS

I had a pretty typical suburban childhood growing up in Waterloo, Iowa. I have two older brothers, Joe and Jake, and a younger sister, Lindsey. We were close as kids, but we also pursued our own interests and went our separate ways a lot of the time. In one thing, though, we were completely united. We pestered our parents, George and Sandy, nonstop, about getting a dog.

Ever since I could remember, I couldn't get enough of hanging out with other people's dogs. As a result, I got to see dogs that were pets and dogs that were working animals and some dogs that were both. At this point, all I knew was that I was a kid that liked being around dogs. I had no idea that this was the beginning of my education about canine behavior and my first glimpses at the unique bonds humans form with dogs. I had no idea, either, that one day I would have a career that revolved about dogs and that very bond.

We had friends and neighbors who had dogs, mostly bird dogs that retrieved the birds their owners hunted. I joined our friends' duck and pheasant hunts and was fascinated by the dogs' amazing athletic abilities and their desire to seek out and retrieve a kill. I marveled at their willingness to endure harsh temperatures, thick undergrowth, and other obstacles to get the job done. I wondered what motivated them and could not have been more impressed by their drive and desire.

I also got to spend a fair bit of time with farm dogs, since Waterloo is pretty close to rural farm country. My dad's side of the family had a farm on the outskirts of town, and I'd go and ride tractors, pick vegetables, and check out the various farm dogs. They weren't working dogs, strictly speaking, but they weren't typical house pets either. They basically had to survive out on the farm on their own, and they did a good job of it. From watching them and the bird dogs, I developed the idea that dogs should be useful and that they were often happiest when they had some kind of job to do—whether it was retrieving for a hunter or taking down a critter for themselves.

I can still picture some of those farm dogs, trotting along, their noses in the air scenting for prey. They'd stop and go stock-still and then pounce into two feet of snow and come up with a field mouse or something else. The way they carried themselves as they proudly bore away their prize said something about what was going on inside them. Of course, on a farm, that kind of prey drive had to be discouraged sometimes. I spent a lot of time dogproofing the chicken coop and keeping dogs away from it and the hens inside. I learned, early on, that dogs are genetically designed to be very good at tracking things and using their noses as a guide.

——————

When I was in the sixth grade, my parents finally came home one day with a black Labrador retriever puppy we gave the not-so-original name of Bud. From the time Bud was old enough to walk a few hundred yards to the time I left for the navy at the age of seventeen, I loved walking with him. Sometimes it was just a few hundred yards, and sometimes it was hours-long walks through the streets and also in the fields, where I walked with Bud while he was out hunting with my dad.

Bud was, well, he was my boy. I'd come home from school every day and there he was, waiting for me, eager as all get-out to go outside with me. I wasn't a complete loner, but I also wasn't the most outgoing kid around, so Bud and I spent a lot of time together, and I talked with him a lot, especially when I was younger. I loved sports but was a bit of a runt; I didn't develop fully until after most everybody else my age had and was somewhat self-conscious about it. Bud didn't ever mind, though, and he never let me down, and all that just made him an even better companion.

That's not to say that Bud lacked the qualities of those good hunting dogs our neighbors and friends had. Just like with them, I was blown away by Bud's ability to detect different scents. I would be out walking with him, and he'd do his usual nose-to-the-ground thing, occasionally rising up to sniff the air, and then all of a sudden he'd switch from going in one direction to moving in another. His entire demeanor would change, and he'd run over to some area and start digging through layers of snow and ice until he uncovered some fast-food hamburger wrapper that had been buried there for who knows how long. The power of a dog's sense of smell always fascinated me.

With Bud I also saw a dog's intelligence at work all the time, but especially as it pertained to my Grandma Bev. Whenever she came by the house, Bud would grab something—a sock, a kitchen towel, the TV remote—and bring it to her. Why? Because she always rewarded him with a treat. Bud knew who the easy marks were, and he took full advantage of them. Actually, it was hard to know who was happier with the whole thing, Bud or Grandma Bev. Even as a kid, I sensed that if you gave a dog some of what he wanted—in this case, a treat—you could get a whole lot of what you wanted from a dog, such as companionship.

That's not to say that Bud's companionship didn't come without its glitches. I remember the night when my dad came home late and was limping pretty badly. He had wrestled quite a bit in his younger days and now had bad knees and hips as a result of too many double-leg takedowns. On this particular day, Dad had been out with Bud at a local golf course, and Bud had come charging at him with great exuberance. He had accidentally clipped my dad and sent him sprawling into the snow. My father lay there, flat on his back, in pretty serious pain for quite a while.

I remember being at home, wondering where he and Bud had gone. When my dad came home and explained what had happened, he told me that after Bud knocked him down, the dog knew that something wasn't right. So he came and stood right by my dad, offering whatever consolation and comfort he could. That was the part of the story I liked—it was yet another example of the 100 percent loyalty you get from a dog when you two form a bond.

— 3 —

A DESIRE TO SERVE AND DEFEND

Both my grandfathers served in World War II, one in the army and one in the navy. They didn't talk much about their war experiences, but I was eager to hear about them and listened avidly to anything they shared about their time in the military. I can't say exactly why I was so interested, but I was, more so than most other members of my family.

I became fascinated—"obsessed" might be a better word—with the idea of becoming a U.S. Navy SEAL team member after reading an article about them in *Popular Mechanics* magazine. The movie *Navy SEALs* inspired me as well. I later found out that this film was an unintentional but effective recruiting tool that helped not only me but a number of other guys on my team decide to enlist.

Because of my grandfathers and also because of my father's influence, I was raised to believe that you should be proud to be an American and that you can do a lot more than just express that pride verbally. My response to those stories I heard and the words I read and the images I saw was to want to go out into the world and do something active for my country.

I also had a highly refined sense of right and wrong instilled in me. On one day in particular—January 6, 1992, to be exact—that sense came sharply into play. It was a Friday afternoon, and I was a freshman in high school. I was a new member of the swim team, and as part of an initiation ritual I was required to wear my Speedo swimsuit over my jeans. The goal was to see if "newbies" could handle the inevitable snickering and wisecracks, but things escalated way beyond that.

I was walking to class, just after having lunch with my brother Jake, when I ran into a gauntlet of students, all of whom happened to be black. Obviously my hazing attire made me stand out from the crowd and could have led to why I was selected for what happened next. I can't say for sure if what did happen was a racially motivated attack, but I do know that racial tensions across the country had been high ever since a black man named Rodney King had been severely beaten by white members of the Los Angeles police force nearly a year before. My racially mixed high school, Waterloo West, was not exempt from the tension. We could all feel it rise up at times. In fact, a Cultural Enrichment Club meeting had recently been canceled because some white students had allegedly been promising to show up and cause problems.

I guess, simply put, I was just in the wrong place at the wrong time. I was beaten up pretty badly, though, and I hated the feeling of powerlessness I experienced in those moments when I was punched, kicked, and slammed into the walls. Absolutely no action was taken against the guys who did it. So *I* took some action. I told myself that I would never again experience that kind of helplessness.

I joined a local dojo, a school for practicing martial arts, led by an excellent sensei, or teacher. My sensei's mentor had served in Vietnam as a Force Reconnaissance Marine, and I was naturally very interested in his combat experiences. I committed myself to learning how to defend myself in a more disciplined and learned way than just some street-fighting moves. While I couldn't have connected all these dots back then, that desire to protect myself against future attacks from bullies dovetailed with what I would come to see as the role of the United States: to protect and defend the country and other people against aggressors.

Add all of those influences up, and throw in a best friend named Matt who shared a similar interest and work ethic, and I was fully committed to joining the navy and the SEALs as my ultimate aspiration.

The Navy SEALs are the elite of the elite. They conduct top-secret operations behind enemy lines. SEAL stands for Sea, Air, and Land, and a Navy SEAL team will use one or any combination of the three approaches to reach their mission location.

— —

At this point, however, I wasn't exactly the model physical specimen that a SEAL team member needs to be. As I mentioned earlier, I was the typical late bloomer physically. However, I was drawn to fitness and the mental and spiritual discipline required by the martial arts.

If I did possess one trait out of the box, so to speak, that made me a prime candidate to be a SEAL team member, it was this: I was ultracompetitive. I hated to lose, and as much as I felt helpless during that attack by virtue of being so outnumbered, I also had the idea in my mind that I should have been able to overcome those odds. In my fantasy, after I had been jumped I would have been able to fight my way out of it, breaking jaws and knocking out teeth along the way.

One trait that successful SEAL team candidates have in common is that they can't stand to lose—and they won't quit. Ever.

— —

Since I knew before I joined the navy that I wanted to be a SEAL, I let the recruiters know that was the case. Not that my desire mattered much, but when it came time for me to take the preliminary screening test, I was well ahead of the game. Because I was so highly motivated, I'd been working out twice a day, six days a week for a long time before reporting to the Great Lakes Naval Training Center. In fact, I thought that basic training was a detriment rather than a benefit for someone like me. The physical training was *less* intense than what I was used to doing, so much so that I felt like it was hurting my fitness level.

Two weeks into basic training, I took the Navy SEAL fitness test. It consists of a 500-yard swim, the maximum number of sit-ups and push-ups you can do in two minutes for each, six dead-hang pull-ups, and a 1.5-mile run. I easily outdid the minimum numbers. Fortunately, that allowed me to do additional workouts and have access to the fitness facilities.

Had I not passed that test—and I was the only one of the eight or nine in my division who attempted it—I wouldn't have been bounced out of the navy, but I would have felt like I had been.

I had been accepted into the SEAL program, but my training for that did not begin right away. First, like everyone else in the navy, I had to complete the eight weeks of basic training. Then I went through four months of training as an intelligence specialist, and then my BUD/S training to be a Navy SEAL began. BUD/S stands for Basic Underwater Demolition/SEAL. I had gone from having a black Labrador and best friend named Bud to being in BUD/S. At this point I had no idea that my love of dogs and desire to serve my country would someday have a much tighter, more life-changing connection than that.

— 4 —

COMBINING PASSIONS

Iraq, April 2003

The ground war was still in its early stages, and my SEAL team platoon was working alongside the 1st Marine Division. We had arrived in Baghdad and shortly afterward were tasked with taking the key city of Tikrit to the northwest. Our convoy consisted of my sixteen-member platoon and twenty-five thousand Marines. We stretched out about 30 miles long as we made our way along the 112-mile route between the two cities.

Before we arrived at Tikrit, we stopped with the convoy to review the final stages of our entry into the city. In an instant we found ourselves under attack from insurgents. A fierce firefight broke out, with antitank, antiaircraft rounds going off, the *whip-whip* sound of returned gunfire whizzing over our heads, and 84 mm rockets being launched into a field just outside the city. We successfully fought off the ambush and continued on our way, on high alert.

We joined a coordinated approach to the city that included the 2nd Battalion, Light Armored Reconnaissance, and Light Armored Vehicles. When we entered Tikrit we did so from all directions. It was one of those moments when the hairs on the back of your neck stand up. The streets were deserted. There was no sign of activity anywhere, but you knew, especially after the ambush on the road, that there were pockets of resistance lurking in the city. Maybe, even as we arrived, insurgents were watching us and waiting for an opportunity.

We arrived at Saddam Hussein's presidential palace complex, where we met with limited resistance. The building was so massive, it took us more than an hour to clear and secure all the rooms. Hussein had already fled the city and was on the run.

My platoon was in the palace for four days. We spent part of that time on the roof, which was the highest point in the city. From there we could see the Tigris River and beyond to the airfield where hundreds of pounds of cached weapons and munitions had been destroyed by U.S. Air Force bombers with JDAMs and other smart bombs. As we sat on the roof, we watched sympathetic detonations going off all day and all night—explosives accidentally set off by nearby explosions—providing a sound-and-light show to an otherwise still but seething city.

One night, I was on the roof doing my four-hour block between 0200 and 0600 when I saw three little flashes of light go off about 350 yards away. A few seconds later three big explosions followed. The flashes and explosions continued, advancing to within 100 yards of the palace. As I was getting on the radio, I saw an army counterartillery unit fire up across the Tigris. That movement was followed by the noise of heavy weapons fire. In a matter of seconds those flashes of light we'd seen erupted into one massive flash as the army counterartillery unit hit its target. I sat there and wondered what might have happened if those insurgents had not been wiped off the map.

Those "what if" questions are always a part of war, of course, but you don't spend a whole lot of time thinking about the answers. All I knew was that I was grateful that the army battery had been posted so nearby. A few weeks into our operation, we had another valuable "weapon" at our disposal. Several MWDs arrived to assist the marine forces.

As the weeks passed, life took on a kind of routine—a combat nor-malcy that had you hypervigilant and never fully able to rest at any time. We had no FOB established, no outposts, and no real secu-rity perimeter. We spent nights sleeping under Humvees and eventually set up tents beneath large camouflage-netting hills we constructed. An hour of sleep here, and a twenty-minute nap there, was about all the shut-eye anyone got. Nearly every moment was punctuated by gunfire, shouts, or some other disruption. We'd all endured sleep deprivation before, but this time it was definitely taking its toll.

The clearing operations we were doing to neutralize mines and remove other obstacles were particularly difficult. The poten-tial for these operations to become mind-numbing was certainly there, due largely to the combination of the repetitive nature of this work, our lack of sleep, and even the absence of basic creature comforts. Clearing operations are highly dangerous, but they are also, obviously, of critical importance.

At one point, we were in a more rural area outside the city, and I observed as a small group of marines came upon a small cavelike structure. It was a kind of hut with a very small entrance. We'd all encountered other structures similar to that one and had al-ready searched thousands of buildings without any issues. The natural inclination might be to assume that everything was okay here as well, but we all knew we could never give in to that kind of thinking.

This platoon had been assigned an explosive-detection dog, and he and his handler went up to the hut's doorway. Immediately, the dog alerted—his ears went up and he sat down. I was on the security perimeter and watched all this through a pair of binoculars.

Later, talking to the marines who had investigated that cave, I learned that a grenade booby trap had been set in that doorway. The dog detected the explosives. Sitting down was his way to alert his handler that explosives were present. Because of the way the structure was situated, and because of the way the explosives were placed, without question, the first two or three marines going in would have been killed. The next one or two behind them probably would have been injured fairly badly. This incident was literally and figuratively life-changing.

Seeing for myself how that dog had just gone about his business and had instantly identified the danger, and then hearing more about it, made me want to never go anywhere without a dog out ahead of me ever again. Explosives, IEDs, booby traps, and trip wires are all easy to place and sometimes hard for humans to detect. At the pace that we were moving, it was impossible to sweep everywhere with a metal detector or have an Explosive Ordnance Disposal (EOD) guy pull open the ground. It's not going to happen. A metal detector doesn't cover everything anyway, because some of the devices use plastic or wood to house the explosives, so there's no metal to detect.

I also realized this: Had there been somebody 20 feet inside that hut with an AK ready to shoot those marines as soon as they came in, the dog would have alerted them to that, too. Many other times on duty in Iraq, I would come to witness the incredible ability that these dogs have to detect explosives, smell human beings in hiding, and hear and smell other sources of danger.

I also recognized something else about these dogs that makes them effective fighters. Unlike us, they don't really know they are in a foreign environment, and that works to their advantage. In some respects, they don't know whether they are in training in the United States or in combat zones overseas. The mountains of Afghanistan or the deserts of Iraq aren't any more out of the dogs' routine than the mountains east of San Diego. They're all mountains with steep, jagged rocks. For them, the only difference in Afghanistan and Iraq is the constant presence of excessively loud noises. Even then, the dogs remain focused and concentrate on sniffing out explosive odors or people as they have been trained to do.

Watching that dog alert the marines to the booby-trapped hut was a "lightbulb" moment for me. I immediately saw a way to combine my passion for protecting and defending people with my lifelong passion for and fascination with dogs. I wanted to better comprehend dogs' amazing abilities and work to harness them so the dogs could become effective weapons against the tools of modern warfare. I wanted to train dogs for Navy SEAL teams and other parts of the military. Eventually, that's just what I did.

— —

I spent years operating with SEAL Team Three based out of Coronado, in San Diego, completing multiple deployments to the Middle East. I loved every minute of it. It was an incredibly intense, fast-paced, and rewarding career that challenged me constantly but made me realize who I was.

The men that I worked and served with as a member of SEAL Team Three were an incredibly diverse bunch of guys, but we did have some things in common. Many of us were raised in either suburban or rural areas, and the majority of us liked "outdoor enthusiast" activities: hunting, fishing, climbing, hiking, and so on. Almost all of us had played some sort of organized sports.

On the other hand, some guys I met in my time made me do a mental double take and think, *You did* what *before joining up?* For example, in my first platoon, there was a guy who had been an Ivy Leaguer, a Columbia University grad. He had been a Wall Street investor for several years, got bored, decided to quit, and joined the navy. He was thirty-one years old when he went through BUD/S. I'd also been on a team with a guy who had previously been a rodeo clown.

Eventually I left SEAL Team Three and went to be an advanced training instructor at SEAL Qualification Training. I spent about eighteen months there, and during a training trip to a desert environment I contracted valley fever. Valley fever is a fungal infection that spreads in your lungs like mold and scars your lung tissue permanently, causing you to lose lung capacity. After recovering from that as much as my body was capable of, I transferred over to BUD/S to be an instructor. I spent almost four years there selecting, teaching, and forging some of the finest warriors our nation has to offer. I have always admired what the SEALs bring to the table as a force protection enhancement, and during that time I learned as much as I could about it.

— • —

Meanwhile, in 2004, as U.S. military activity in Afghanistan and Iraq intensified, the SEALs had begun to use specially trained dogs to meet the specific needs of the Navy SEAL teams. The use of MWDs has evolved around the world over time (for a brief overview of the history of canines in combat prior to this, see the appendix at the back of the book), but what SEAL teams in these two conflicts especially needed was Special Operations Forces (SOF) dogs that could be trained to sniff out explosives, just like that dog had done for its marine unit at that little hut outside Tikrit, Iraq. They also needed dogs that could detect and apprehend the enemy.

Trainers, breeders, and handlers use lots of different methods to train dogs and have lots of different opinions about the best way to do so, but there is one thing they all agree on, and that is this: Dogs are better detection tools than any machines—be it for sniffing out explosives or using their extraordinary sense of smell to locate enemy troops or snipers. There have been numerous attempts to build machines that can replicate what a dog's nose does, but to this point, none of them have come close.

At first, the demand for dogs far outweighed the supply, as the SEAL K-9 program was essentially starting from scratch. At the same time, other branches of the military—as well as many U.S. cities, in the wake of 9/11—were looking to ramp up their use of explosive-detection dogs. One way to obtain dogs quickly was to get them from the regular military, where patrol dogs and detection dogs were already being used, but it quickly became apparent that there was a substantial difference between how MWDs operated and what SOF dogs needed to do. The tactical movements of a SEAL team required SOF dogs that were trained to function at higher speeds and at a more advanced level, for instance, than dogs working for the military police.

Navy SEAL dogs needed unique training, and as with most things to do with SEAL teams, be it technology or tactics, SEAL Team Six pioneered the way. They created and refined the canine program, and their training procedures and other elements of SOF canines trickled down to the East Coast and West Coast teams.

As I was leaving the navy in 2009, the SEAL canine program was going into even higher gear in and around Coronado, California. I'd already purchased property and had plans in place to create the best dog-training facility I could. My eleven years as a SEAL team member and other experiences allowed me to begin my business with contracts to train SOF dogs. I am proud to train highly skilled multipurpose dogs that succeed downrange, and am grateful that I can continue to contribute to the SEALs' ongoing efforts, however indirectly.

Those of us who train SOF canines are a very small and very tight-knit community. We assist one another in every way we can. We sometimes trade dogs among ourselves when the need arises. There's no room for us to let ego or dollars get in the way of succeeding at job one—training dogs who will save the lives of our brothers in combat.

PART II

ON MAKING THE GRADE

5

NOT YOUR TYPICAL HOUSE PET

The dogs that we procure and train for the SEALs are all herding dogs—pointy-eared shepherds, usually Dutch Shepherds or Belgian Malinois. A herding dog is any of a variety of different breeds that historically have helped farmers herd groups of animals such as sheep. Herding dogs are working dogs, and they need to have a job to do.

Chopper, the ex-SOF dog that saved Brett and his platoon from insurgents in Iraq, is a Belgian Malinois. The breed gets its name from both the country (Belgium) and the city (Malines) where they were first bred. Although the breed's history extends back earlier, it was first registered in Belgium and in France in 1891. There are four different varieties, or coat colors and patterns, of Malinois, but many of them are beige with a black mask. They look, at first glance, a lot like the more commonly known German shepherd, but the Malinois is a lighter, leaner dog.

A dedicated early group of breeders and trainers in Europe refined the breed so that it is prized not only for its work ethic but also for its intelligence, stamina, and trainability. According to the American Kennel Club (AKC) the Belgian Malinois was first registered in the United States in 1911, but it has always been one of the breeds with the smallest number of registrants. For instance, only 107 dogs were registered with the AKC in the ten years between 1959 and 1969. While they do enjoy a nearly fanatical following here, they are still relatively rare.

Because they do have a long history of breeding, training, and competing in Europe, we most often import the Malinois we train for the military. There are some very good breeders and trainers here, but we want to be able to take advantage of those long ancestral lines and the rich tradition found in dogs from Belgium, Holland, and elsewhere. It would take generations and generations and countless dollars to begin a selective breeding program using those bloodlines here in the United States and we just don't have the time to wait. We'd rather sacrifice the "Made in the USA" label than potentially lose American lives or waste taxpayer dollars. As it is, the navy invests well over $50,000 in the acquisition, training, and care of a single dog, like Chopper, before the animal gets deployed with his handler. The bottom line is that we all want the best for our troops, and at this point that means importing the dogs from overseas.

It is important to point out that when I acquire a Malinois from a European breeder, I'm not getting a very young puppy that hasn't been trained at all. The dog is already about two to three years old and has gone through rigorous training. Some of the dogs even have become what is referred to as "titled dogs." That means that they've not only been trained but have also earned certification in one of several different European dog sports. One of the better known of these is *Schutzhund*, a dog sport popular in Germany. Originally, a dog that had completed *Schutzhund* training and had become certified in the sport was also essentially qualified to become a German police dog. That is no longer necessarily the case, partially because the sport is so popular that many different breeds now enter and compete.

Schutzhund competition results reveal to what degree dogs possess traits like courage, intelligence, perseverance, and the protective instinct. There are three levels of achievement, and the tests cover three aspects of the dog's abilities: tracking, obedience, and protection. A dog must pass all three phases of the test in order to receive certification and become titled.

So the dogs we acquire have already earned some measure of distinction. Typically, they have had some obedience training and some bite work (including controlled bite work, where they have to release their grip on command) and have completed an article search/tracking exercise that requires them to go through numerous obstacles and then find a person or an object.

While this all sounds good in theory, and there are obvious benefits to acquiring dogs with this kind of training, problems can arise because each dog's original trainer had his or her own way of doing things. We may come back with five titled dogs, but because each trainer used different methods we have to retrain the dogs to do things our way. In some cases the dogs recognize another language for commands, and most often we continue to use that language. For example, the *"Reviere"* and *"Braafy,"* commands that Brett used with Chopper are Dutch words.

— • —

What exactly makes an individual dog, be it a Belgian Malinois or another breed, the right dog to be a Navy SEAL dog? It takes a combination of different physical traits and specific qualities of temperament. The dropout/failure rate among humans who want to qualify as Navy SEALs is very high. The rate among the dogs we select and train is even higher.

The single most desirable quality in a dog that will do SOF work has to do with temperament. It happens to be the same for humans who want to be Navy SEALs: They just won't quit.

A dog must be physically fit, well bred, and well trained, but it must also be highly motivated and extremely energetic. To put this in some context, think of the most ball-crazy dog you've ever seen. You know the type, the one who will pursue a ball faster, for greater amounts of time, and with a maniacal determination that seems endless. Well, to make it through the program and qualify to join the SEAL teams on their missions, dogs must be even *more* energetic, focused, and relentless.

Here's the analogy I often use to describe the difference between a ball-crazy dog and a Navy SEAL dog. A lot of people want to be professional athletes. They start playing a sport early on. A few of them become big-deal high school athletes, and even fewer go on to play in college. A very, very small percentage of those athletes realize their dream to play professionally. From *that* select group who make it into Major League Baseball, the National Basketball Association, the National Football League, or another pro sport league, an even more minute percentage become stars, Hall of Famers, legends. Every dog we work with is as physically gifted as a LeBron James or a Michael Phelps.

Obviously, though, great athletes are great for more reasons than their physical abilities alone. They are tenacious competitors, driven by something inside them that wants to not just succeed but dominate. That doesn't mean that they are arrogant or malicious— they just want to be better than you or anyone else. The Belgian Malinois I work with have to have that component. They have to have some inner fire that you can control and unleash to the best advantage.

That inner fire can be described as enthusiasm or tenacity. It's what a coach looking to recruit an athlete looks for, and it's what I look for in an SOF dog. In a dog I call it "drive." It is the combination of their unwillingness to quit and their willingness to go after something like a ball unrelentingly that I look for when evaluating dogs. It may sound like the same thing, but the example that follows should shed some light on the differences between not quitting and really going after it.

For most pet owners, the drive I'm talking about can best be observed when you have in your possession a favorite toy that your dog likes to play with. For a lot of dogs, the toy of choice is a tennis ball. When I go to look at dogs, physically mature dogs in most cases, what I want to see is behaviors that would drive most pet owners nuts. The dog should express its desire in leaping, barking, turning, and spinning—not just for a little while but persistently, for a long period of time. The dog's desire must be over the top, and it literally exhibits that trait by jumping up to nearly my eye level to get to that ball. The dog is, as I said, relentless, and would very definitely cross the line between what we consider acceptable and unacceptable pet behavior. I want to see a dog that is willing and able to use its only real weapon—its mouth—to get that ball. Simply put, the dog must have so much desire and be so unwilling to give in and lose the battle for that ball that it will actually bite a human to get it.

If you've ever seen a dog that just shivers with excitement and pent-up desire to get a toy, then you have some idea of what I'm talking about. It's as if every fiber of that dog's being is twitching with its built-in, hardwired desire to get at the ball, which it sees as prey. For the dogs at the top of my list, the object of desire is nearly immaterial. I could be holding a piece of pipe, a length of rebar, a stick, it doesn't matter. The dog wants whatever it is and will do nearly anything to get it.

In addition to wanting it while it's in your possession, the dog will tear off after the object at high speed as soon as you throw it. The aggressive pursuit of that object, the speed at which the dog goes after it, is off the charts. To say that the dog goes after it is an understatement. Rather, the dog launches itself like a rocket.

When the dog reaches the object, it plants its forelegs so forcefully that its hind legs rise up off the ground, kicking dust and debris all over the place. The dog will then grab the object, wrap its front legs and paws around it, and assume a guarding position, not allowing anyone near its prize.

Compare that response to your typical ball-obsessed dog and I think you get the picture. Prey drive is the ability and desire to chase and catch anything that moves. What I'm looking for, as I've said, is over-the-top, extreme prey drive. The dogs have to be bold, powerful, stubborn, and dominant. In addition, and perhaps most importantly, they have to be absolutely crazy about retrieving things.

Now, if you approach the dog once it has successfully retrieved an object and try to take that object away, you will encounter fierce resistance. Of course, I'm talking about a dog's raw ability at this point. Eventually that dog will have to be trained to pursue an object with this kind of abandon only on command, and also learn to relinquish it when told to do so.

I've taken clients who want a personal protection dog to view candidates, and when they see that kind of raw behavior they frequently ask, "Is there something wrong with that dog?"

I always answer, "No. There's a lot right with that dog."

That kind of nearly out-of-control pursuit is needed because frequently these working dogs, once in the field, have to charge into unknown environments, and just as frequently, ones that present a real danger to them. You don't want dogs that are going to hesitate at all. They absolutely must remain task focused and able to block out all distractions. The ones that we deploy have to be unflappable in all circumstances. They can't be spooked by dark rooms, slippery floors, open metal grating, helicopters, fast-roping, rappelling, parachuting, entering and exiting water, jumping onto unstable objects, or entering tight places like ducts and crawl spaces. Not only can't they be spooked, they have to go into those places and do those activities willingly and with confidence and purpose, as evidenced by their upright carriage, their scorpion tails curling over their backs, their pricked ears, and their chests thrust forward, no matter how foreign or unfamiliar a situation they are in. They need to stroll in everywhere like they own the place and do the job. In other words, they need to act just like their human counterparts.

———

One of the main jobs that a Navy SEAL dog is trained to do is apprehension. Under combat conditions a dog is often required to find and apprehend a specific object and/or the enemy.

In terms of apprehending—that is, cornering or holding on to an enemy—which a dog often physically does by using its mouth and biting down as hard as is needed, a dog has to have an inbred ability to be aggressive toward humans. I want to make this point as clear as possible. Animals can demonstrate aggression toward other animals or toward people. Just because a dog is aggressive toward animals doesn't mean it has aggression toward people, and vice versa. I believe there is a great misconception in our society over this point. There's no correlation between those two types of aggression.

Belgian Malinois dogs can be human aggressive. They have a strong willingness to be assertive and to bite. That makes sense considering that they were bred to watch over flocks of animals and protect them from rustlers. Through selective breeding, the herding dogs we "recruit" have had that human aggression tweaked to a very high degree out of necessity. It takes proper training and control by a well-trained handler to keep these dogs from posing a potential threat to ordinary folks.

The SEAL teams, unlike some other agencies, have to employ dual-purpose dogs. Not only must the dogs excel at apprehension, they also need to excel at detection. A lot of the work these dogs do is detection work—finding people, explosives, narcotics, and other things. In fact, they need to detect something in order to apprehend it, and they detect things mostly with their noses.

Dogs are legendary, and for good reason, for the sensitivity of their noses. Scientists estimate that, on average, a dog has 220 million scent receptors in its nose. The average person has 5 million.

I frequently say, when describing what I'm looking for in a dog, that I want a nose and the rest of the dog that comes with it doesn't really matter. That's not literally true, of course, but it does come close to describing the priority I place on a dog's olfactory ability. I term a dog's ability and desire to find an object that isn't visible "hunt drive." That means that whether an object is thrown into an area where the dog can't see it or the object was hidden previously, I want to see that dog use its nose and not its eyes to locate it. An ideal canine candidate for the Navy SEALs has to possess a hyper prey drive *and* a hyper hunt drive.

When using their hunt drive, instinctively, these dogs will immediately go into a serpentine search pattern or a figure eight. Their noses will either be lowered or up in the air, "reading" scent molecules to locate their object. Just as when they chase and capture something they've seen someone throw, their hunt drive will turn into aggressive possession once they have the object.

Hounds (bloodhounds in particular) are extraordinary trackers, but they lack the prey drive or human aggressiveness that is needed. The same is true with retrievers. Labradors are great at sniffing out drugs, explosives, and munitions. They just don't have the human-aggression component that is necessary to meet the SEAL teams' needs. Belgian Malinois possess both traits necessary to be multipurpose Navy SEAL dogs. I don't just mean they have those two traits—they have them in spades, particularly the dogs that make the grade and get deployed in theater. The breed has a lot of other great attributes: Their athleticism and endurance are extraordinary, and their fearsome appearance certainly helps in some regards, too. However, since a Navy SEAL dog's primary tasks are to detect specific odors and to assist in capturing bad guys, the Malinois' ability and willingness to do those two things make them ideal candidates.

Still, finding an individual dog with both those qualities in the right intensity and balance is truly a one-in-a-thousand (or more) proposition. By necessity, you might make some concessions with a dual-purpose dog that you might not make with a single-purpose dog.

Look at it this way. In baseball, scouts look for five-tool players: those who can hit for average, can hit for power, possess a strong throwing arm, have above-average foot speed, and field a good glove. No player has ever been at the top of the charts in every one of those categories, but the ones the scouts pick are, overall, above the average. What we need in terms of Navy SEAL dogs are first-ballot Hall of Famers who are in the 90th percentile in all the skills and qualities we look for.

— ◆ —

There is one last quality that I look for. A dog has to have a high level of forward aggression. This is more than just being human aggressive. It means the dog is willing to stand up and fight a person and not let that person overpower it. Most dogs, even those selected from elite breeders from around the world, don't have this quality to the degree that is needed. Dogs have been domesticated and bred for so long that this type of dog is a very, very rare animal, like one in ten thousand.

To test for that rarest of qualities, I have to put the dog in an uncomfortable spot and put pressure on him. Essentially, what I'm testing for is his flight-versus-fight response. I want to see him go through that thought process. *Am I going to take this guy on? I know that chances are I'm going to get hurt if I do, so I could bail out.* The dogs that don't bail out, the ones that choose to fight and not flee, are the ones we want.

In evaluating dogs for purchase and further training, I do have an advantage when it comes to testing for this kind of aggressive behavior. They've never seen me before, so I immediately have their attention as a potential threat. I put additional pressure on them by approaching them and keeping my body square to them and making fierce direct eye contact. In some cases I'll present a stick as a weapon and tap them with it, or grab a handful of their skin and squeeze it. I want them to come after me. Of course, I'm wearing a "bite suit" for protection when I do this. Dogs that sink their teeth into that suit are good candidates for selection.

It's important to note that there is a crucial distinction between dogs who will go on the offensive and those who will continue to fight when placed on the defensive. A dog may demonstrate prey drive when going after a squirrel, but ones that will exhibit that same prey drive when squaring off with a moose or other large animal are rare and desirable as working dogs.

— • —

Sometimes, a dog's willingness to go anywhere and do anything can end up being a kind of detriment. That's especially true for a dog that is "fresh out of the box" and at the beginning of its training with us and exposed to new activities and new environments. Belgium isn't exactly a high-desert mountainous region, like the battlefields of Afghanistan often are, so that's one type of environment we need to expose new dogs to. It turns out that the area in San Diego County near the West Coast SEAL teams is a lot like that region. It also includes a plentiful amount of manzanita bushes, which are native to North America and which, therefore, the dogs are also not familiar with.

Manzanita means "little apple" in Spanish, but manzanita bushes don't have apples. Instead they are loaded with thorns that get hold of you and don't let go. Most of us who've endured the agony of working our way through, around, under, and away from a manzanita's thorny grasp think of it as more of a man-eater than an apple.

As a SEAL, you get exposed to manzanita during night patrols, and it is about the thickest, coarsest, sharpest vegetation that you'll ever encounter. When training the dogs doing mountain patrols at night, you sometimes find yourself wishing that these dogs didn't have that all speed-ahead spirit. One dog in particular, Barco, was one of our larger canines, weighing in at 80 pounds. He was a freight train with a brain. Sometimes, however, that locomotive engine in him overpowered the driver.

We were on a night training exercise, and Barco was on a 30-foot retractable leash, a heavy-duty flexi-lead. Short leads are effective in some scenarios, but when training a dog to do detection work in the mountains, they just aren't practical or realistic to use. If you've ever walked your dog and had the frustration of him or her going around a tree and wrapping the lead around it, you've experienced something like what we've endured during these training exercises. Imagine, though, if instead of your mild-mannered dog on a short leash winding around an oak tree with its relatively smooth bark, you've got an 80-pound high-energy beast intent on going around a thorny manzanita bush to get to an odor so that he can get a reward. Add in that your outing isn't along a level sidewalk in a subdivision or city but is in the rocky, uneven mountains. Plus, remember that it's nighttime and there are no streetlights. It is pitch-black—and a classic recipe for disaster.

I've been out with a group of six to eight dogs and their handlers on training exercises that are supposed to be done in stealth, but every few seconds you'd hear another handler swear when one dog after another got tangled up in a man-eating bush. Barco had a real talent for forging ahead, wrapping back around a manzanita bush, doubling back, coming back around, straining against his lead, and wrapping it tighter and tighter around the bush.

On the night I'm referring to, I was out with Barco and his handler and a few others. We came to a downhill section, and Barco suddenly took off like a shot. It was like watching a scene in an old Hollywood Western where a cowboy is being dragged across the ground by his horse. Barco's handler, who shall remain nameless, went down the hill like a rag doll, bumping along and kicking up a cloud of dust, gravity and Barco determining his speed and direction. I went down the hill after them as quickly as I could, but not soon enough to prevent the handler from getting tangled upside down in a prickly manzanita bush. Barco's forward progress was only arrested because his handler's limbs were entwined in that manzanita. Each of Barco's continued thrusts forward impaled his handler more deeply onto the sharp points and further knotted the lead. It required many minutes of patient undoing to free both man and beast.

Sometimes it isn't a dog's over-the-top eagerness that gets handlers in trouble. Sometimes the handlers "mishandle" a situation. Ball rewards are what keep these dogs motivated. Once, one of the handlers, a guy named Matt, and his dog Arras were on a night patrol, and Arras correctly indicated when he came into odor by sitting still and staring at it. To reward him for properly detecting and indicating, Matt thought it was a good idea to toss Arras a ball. Matt had actually forgotten that it was nighttime because he had on his night-vision goggles. Although dogs can see well at night, Arras didn't catch sight of the ball immediately, so he didn't make the catch. Instead, he heard the ball hit off some rock and bounce down the slope. Keep in mind, we were at the top of a 4,800-foot mountain. Arras took off, with Matt at the other end of the leash. Matt was swept off his feet and made it down the rocky slope considerably faster than he'd trudged up it moments before.

I think that in education and in parenting both, incidents like these are teachable moments. So, when you get your lightly-bloodied-and-battered handler back near you, you remind him that in certain situations, it's best to get the dog right by your side and just hand him his reward. With dogs and humans, it's all a learning process. Few of our handlers have any previous experience with a dog with the physical gifts and enormous drive that our future multipurpose K-9s have. All too frequently, they have to learn about this drive the hard way. It's as if they've been playing a pretty competitive game of playground basketball all their lives and suddenly find themselves playing against an NBA squad—that's just how impressive these dogs are physically.

6

WELL TRAINED

In the run-up to Operation Iraqi Freedom in early 2003, I participated in a bit of navy history. As a part of our general maritime
training exercises—you can even go onto the SEALs Web site to
see photos of these drills—we climbed up an oil/gas platform's
superstructure from a Naval Special Warfare (NSW) Rigid Hull
Inflatable Boat (RHIB) piloted by Special Warfare Combatant-
craft Crewmen. We did these training exercises often, but when
we found out that an upcoming mission would actually involve
this kind of work, the training took on a new sense of urgency and
importance for each of us.

Six weeks prior to the onset of the ground warfare, we learned
that we were being tasked with taking over two oil terminals in
the Persian Gulf. This was going to be my first big mission. Because of the restrictions against Iraq put in place by the international community, these two oil terminals had taken on strategic
importance. They were a bit dilapidated, but because of where
they were, the Iraqis had used them increasingly to smuggle oil out
of the country to sell it. Their supertankers would pull up and
then sneak out again loaded with crude oil. The oil ran through
two 48-inch pipelines placed along the floor of the Persian Gulf,

and the two oil rigs were pumping millions of barrels of oil. The U.S. military's concern was that, because the Iraqi regime suspected that the country would soon be invaded, they would blow up the pipelines to prevent their enemies from using the oil and also create a huge environmental disaster and distraction. They would blame us for the resulting explosions, fire, and oil spill and make *us* look like the bad guys.

We also had some intelligence information that the platforms were rigged with explosives and that the Iraqis were going to blow them up as soon as we got on board. At one point we heard that there were over a hundred Iraqi Republican Guards stationed on the rigs and that they were going to stand and die fighting us if we came and tried to take over the platforms.

So it was pretty harrowing, because we had thirty-two guys in a couple of small RHIBs that we were going to ride in on and assault this target. If the intelligence was correct, we were going to be pretty badly outnumbered in one of the best-case scenarios. In the worst-case scenario . . .

Even without knowing all of that, we would have taken our training seriously, but we took it up a few notches. We actually built an exact replica of those platforms, which were separated by several miles of open water. Then we practiced and practiced a coordinated assault on them both, along with a metering station and pipeline manifold many miles away from those two rigs. We had three big targets in all to neutralize at the same time. We figured that the Iraqis would have a communications system in place that would allow them to notify each location to detonate any explosives placed at all three if there was any slipup in the timing on our end.

This mission was, at this point in time, the largest operation in the history of NSW. All of my team—SEAL Team Three—and all eight SEAL platoons were assigned to take down these targets simultaneously. To put it mildly, this mission was a huge logistical nightmare. If we pulled it off, it would be a spectacular success. If we didn't, it would be a spectacular disaster.

The targets were enormous, each nearly a mile long with a docking station at one end and with smaller substations running the length of it—all places where Iraqi soldiers could be hiding out. We knew the place was manned, but we didn't know the exact numbers. I can't tell you how many times we rehearsed that operation, but people learn how to perform through repetition. Overrepetition doesn't exist. We had multiple scenarios, some of which included using two helicopters to aid in the assault. Mentally going over and over the list of what-ifs, and what-to-dos in case those what-ifs occurred, became my waking and sleeping reality.

By the time we set out from a naval base in Kuwait in our heavily armed Mark V boats, I was superexcited and definitely ready—our training couldn't have been any more thorough. Thanks to the superior firepower and cruising speed of the Mark V boats, we made the journey to the RHIB transfer point in two hours.

I was part of the team that stormed one of the oil platforms in the middle of the night. I was one of the main breachers, meaning I used a shotgun to open about thirty metal doors to begin clearing each area. Ultimately, we found twenty-three Iraqi soldiers on board, a mixed bag of Republican Guard and paramilitary, Fedayeen Saddam guys. We also captured a few Iraqi intelligence officers and a couple of their navy divers. Our strike took the Iraqis totally by surprise. They never got to use the explosives or the anti-aircraft artillery piece that was positioned to take out approaching watercraft.

We also discovered a treasure trove of weaponry and ammo. In total, it took six hours to take the whole thing down, including handling and conducting initial interrogation of the Iraqi prisoners. Thanks to our element of surprise, we executed the takeover without a single casualty on our side.

The same was true at the second platform. At the metering station the resistance was even stronger and a few Iraqi soldiers were killed, but again, not a single American casualty, wound, or injury. That's pretty much a raging success in my book, and I was, and remain, extremely proud to have been part of SEAL Team Three's role in setting the tone for what was to come.

Since that night, and given what I do today, I've often wondered how Navy SEAL multipurpose canines might have helped us on that mission. Certainly the mission was a resounding success, but we'd placed our troops in great peril. We all understand that dangerous missions are the name of the game, but I can't help wondering how dogs might have made our jobs a bit easier that night.

When I made the transition to training SEALs and later to training dogs to assist them, that mission played a large role in my motivation and in my understanding of the importance of the work I was doing. I knew firsthand just how important proper training is and how crucial and serious preparation is. I wanted the dogs I trained to be able to meet the high standards of effort and execution that were exhibited that night in 2003. I knew they would have to. Because of that first mission I went on as a SEAL, I was determined that the dogs I trained were going to be like the men they served alongside—ready for anything, anywhere, anytime.

Today I make my living and stake my reputation on training dogs. Also, as a former SEAL team member, I take very seriously the responsibilities that the dogs and their handlers shoulder. I couldn't live with myself if I knew that I didn't do everything in my power to make certain that the dogs I provide live up to the standards expected of SEAL team dogs. Lives depend on it.

It helps that I know that the dogs I've trained are going to be rigorously tested. When the SEALs come to test my dogs, they're going to throw everything and the kitchen sink at them to make sure that the dogs are what they need. If there is a single flaw in one of these dogs, they're going to find it. So you have to set these dogs up for success or they're not going to be the best. I never heard my parents say, "That's good enough." I wasn't raised that way, and the SEALs didn't train me to think that way. The SEAL operators deserve, as they say, "nothing but the best for the best."

The great genetic background of the Belgian Malinois isn't enough on its own. The dogs all need to go through rigorous training in order to become qualified to work with SEAL teams. It takes hard work with no shortcuts on the part of both handler and canine, though I believe that the dogs actually enjoy the training work. They get to exhibit the traits that their breed was refined to produce and to give expression to their true nature. What can be better than that?

Δ

The key to training and working with a dog is to establish a bond of trust between you and him. I do that with puppies from the very beginning, and you can also do that with dogs you acquire at later stages in their lives. Dogs learn by association, and I want them to associate me with all the good things in their lives: the food they eat, the water they drink, the things they play with, the exercise they do, and on and on. One simple thing I do to establish that bond and their association with me as a source of positive things is to feed them and give them water myself. I may take it away from them briefly, not to tease them but to get them to understand through repetition "Hey, this guy is the one who gives me what I want."

Repetition is a key part of how dogs learn through association. For example, if you reach into your pocket and pull out a treat that you then present to the dog, he begins to understand that something good comes out of you reaching into your pocket. Through enough repetitions of that action, the association gets hardwired in the dog's brain. This is true to the point that if, after the dog learns to associate your hand going into your pocket with a treat, you pull out a set of keys instead, he will still initially make the same association as before—"I'm getting a treat." Only after you allow the dog to see and sniff the keys (or other objects) and repeatedly *not* reward him after you pull keys or other things out of your pockets will he figure out the difference.

In addition to building trust, we also offer dogs abundant praise when they do things right, be it when they find the ball buried in a tub of bottles or they get to the food dish or whatever. Praise is essential to getting these dogs—or any dog, for that matter—to do what you want. Praise can come in the form of words or a treat or anything that the dog sees as positive. For a dog, a reward of any kind means "I did something good, so I should keep doing that so I keep getting rewarded."

Have you ever heard the expression "It's not what you say but how you say it?" Well, that's true with dogs because, of course, they don't understand the meaning of words; they simply associate the words we use with them, through repetition and reward, with an action or an object. If you wanted to, for instance, you could teach your dog to lie down by using the words "get up." Dogs respond to the sounds we use more than the words themselves. They react even more to your tone. Anyone who has ever had a dog can tell you that if you use an excited, encouraging tone with the dog, he will respond in kind. If you yell at the dog and sound angry, the dog will respond to the tone of your voice even if you are screaming "You're a good boy." The words "bad" and "no" have no real meaning by themselves to a dog—it's all in how you say them. So praise as a reward is not about the words you use but definitely how you say the words.

Dogs read body language much better than they respond to verbal language. This may be because they have a whole nonverbal, postural language they use with each other. Have you ever seen two dogs walking on the street encounter each other? The sniffing and posturing process begins at once. One dog will place his head near or above the other dog's neck and shoulders. The other dog stands up taller and holds itself rigid; its ears either lie flat or more likely stand up. That dog is sending a clear message by making itself appear larger. It is telling the other dog, "You're not going to mess with me." Sometimes one dog will make itself appear smaller; it will lower its hind legs, lay its ears flat, and generally assume a very passive posture.

Dogs apply what they know about canine body language to their physical interactions with people. Here's an example of what I mean. I have a few retired MWDs living at my place. People who are interested in adopting them come by, and many times these people often bend down to try to enter the crate or kennel to greet the dog. I immediately stop them and tell them to try to imagine this scenario from a different perspective. I tell them to imagine that they are in a 10′ × 10′ prison cell. Someone comes into the cell. He's bigger and making some sounds that you don't understand. Then he wants to wrap his arms around you like you're old buddies. What are you going to do? How are you going to respond? I try to make sure people understand very clearly the specific characteristics of working dogs and how they may differ from pets. Being cornered this way in their own space by a stranger can trigger the fight-versus-flight response in these dogs. It's no surprise if they choose to come out fighting.

— · —

When I train a dog all the above-mentioned elements are working together: association, repetition, rewards, and verbal and nonverbal language. I also use a clicker during training to mark behaviors. A clicker is just what it sounds like, an object you hold in your hand that makes a clicking sound when you press it. It's a simple kind of association tool that allows me to communicate to the dog that the behavior he's just exhibited was a proper and acceptable one. In the beginning, when I'm working with a dog, I'll hold a treat in my hand. I sit there looking at the dog and he looks at me. I click and then give him the treat. The dog starts to realize that the clicker sound is a good thing; it leads to a treat. If he does what I want, I click and he gets a treat. So, naturally, the dog starts to offer up behaviors, hoping that one of them will get me to click and then reward him. Like people, dogs learn to perform through repetition. After a while, I don't even have to give the dog a command. He knows what behavior I'm looking for. For example, I click and reward him if he goes into full down position when I want him to. If I want to teach him to bark on command, I wait until he barks, and then I click and reward.

As another example, if I want to get a dog to go into his crate, I place a crate in the middle of a clear room with no other distractions. If the dog takes a step toward that crate, I click and reward him. If he takes another step, I repeat the process, and we keep going that way. When we get to more complicated tasks I use the same process. With the crate, after we repeat that often enough, the dog will go in the room, see the crate, dash into it, lie down, and wait for his treat/reward. This is a win-win. The dog gets a treat and I get the desired outcome. This type of training is called positive reinforcement.

I could go about training dogs a whole other way. I could put a prong collar on a dog and have no treats, and I could get to the same place by punishing the dog for not doing what I wanted him to do. There are still some trainers who use the old spiked, electric-shock choke collar approach. The collar has a remote control the trainer uses to shock the dog. Some trainers also use spiked training collars—with the spikes *inside* the collars, next to dogs' necks—and a whip, a stick, or any other tool to mete out punishment to show the dogs who's boss. A dog gets punished when he doesn't do what he is asked to do. A dog will learn pretty quickly if you train him this way, but it will be at a great cost to the dog. You've now shifted the training away from being about positive reinforcement and turned it into negative reinforcement. You'll wind up with a dog that is doing what he's "supposed" to do because he doesn't want to be punished. This kind of training is, in a sense, an act of coercion—you force an animal to do what you want it to do, instead of letting it do what it naturally wants to do. With the training methods I use, you get a dog that is doing the right thing because he wants to, because he wants that reward. My training methods build trust; training through negative reinforcement destroys it.

Between 90 and 95 percent of the time, when training dogs—

The author, two weeks before joining the Navy, atop the World Trade Center in NYC, aptly wearing a SEAL T-shirt.

The author and "Bud," the dog that started it all.

The author in headdress in central Iraq.

The author on patrol with the acrobat-ninja dog Luke.

The author in front of the U.S.S. *Cole* after it was attacked in Yemen.

SEAL Team Three Echo platoon, after the oil platform takedown operation and two days before the ground war started in Iraq.

The author with Barco, the
uphill-runaway-freight-train of a dog.

Wayne doing what he does best.

Lloyd with Cairo.

Lloyd and Cairo on watch.

Lloyd sending Cairo off to grab an insurgent.

Training in
bitework; notice
the deep full
grip of the
dog's mouth.

Aaron and Castor after detonating one of Castor's life-saving finds.

Dave and Samson,
winning hearts and minds.

The social nature of
these dogs is of the
utmost importance.

Samson and the famous Elmo toy that became his favorite.

Dave and Samson getting some much-needed rest.

MULTI PURPOSE CA[I

Aaron and Castor pose next to the company logo.

Treadmills aren't just for humans.

Wayne and Luke, taking a break during a long training exercise.

The author during a sequence of events from the window training scenario that didn't quite go as planned.

An MWD and his handler getting ready to do some helo operations.

Gearing up for some cold weather detection exercises.

The "company" logo.

Luke smiling at
the photographer.

Dave and Samson getting ready to load
up and get after it.

Samson playing the role
of "hood ornament."

MWD and handler
getting ready to clear
an Afghan village.

Cairo gets his workout
in for the day.

Too cool for school . . .

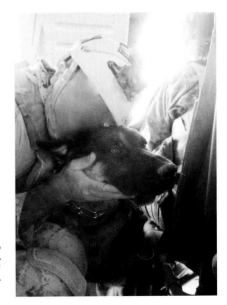

Another dog/handler team,
Curt and Odin, after a long
night of work.

MWD and his handler fresh off an Afghan operation.

Retired MWD with his handler on a wintery R & R hike.

MWD and his handler on a CH-47 helo during insert.

MWD and his handler after a long night of combat operations in Afghanistan.

Arko, the retired but still very capable dog, who was wounded in battle and is now almost ten years old.

The author with Carlos, the dog that protected his handler even when his own life was in the balance.

Curt and Odin preoperation.

Curt and Odin getting
ready to clear a tunnel.

Odin charging ahead,
sniffing out the enemy.

Odin showing off his goggles,
a much-needed piece of gear
to combat the dust and sand
for our K9s.

Odin on a
munitions cache hunt.

Odin ready to go
as usual.

Odin alerting on an
explosive find.

Curt and Odin about to load up for a raid.

An MWD and his handler atop a mountain.

Circling the wagons and getting some much-deserved rest after a long patrol.

either pups or adolescents in early or advanced training stages—I use positive reinforcement. Just as the Navy SEALs are a team and watch out for one another in every way because of their mutual trust and respect, the same has to be true of how a MWD and his handler operate.

Training until we have the necessary results takes time. Once dogs enter into our advanced training, even though they're already titled, it may take one to two years before they are ready to be deployed. That's a lot of time and innumerable repetitions before they are truly ready to do the important work they need to do.

Besides my respect for and love of dogs, and the value we place on the human-canine bond, I spend so much time using positive reinforcement simply because I can't imagine how awful my day would be if I spent the vast majority of it punishing a dog. I can't imagine the toll that would take on me and the dog. Still, it's no wonder that I sometimes see people, both those in the MWD community as well as private pet owners, let their emotions get the better of them. One of the most frequent mistakes I see people make with their dogs is that when "correcting" them, they get the dogs to stop doing what they didn't want them to do and then continue to berate or punish the dog anyway. That's incredibly confusing for a dog. He's thinking, "You told me to stop, I stopped, and now you're still screaming at me or correcting me. Does that mean that you don't want me to do what I'm doing *now*?"

When people do this with pets, they end up with dogs that simply aren't clear about what's expected of them. That's not good. With working dogs, when excessive punishment is used, you end up with either a dog that is aggressive to its handler or a dog that is broken in spirit. We need dogs with intense spirits to take on the challenges of being outstanding detection and apprehension dogs. As I've pointed out before, the pool of suitable dogs is relatively small. To see a dog with the right characteristics ruined by poor training methods is both heartbreaking and an enormous waste of a valuable resource.

I cannot stress enough how the use of punishment can break

the spirit of a dog. That's especially true of dogs that are just entering adulthood, the prime age for specialized training. It seems counterintuitive to me that we select and breed dogs to have a fierce and courageous demeanor and then try to take that spirit away from them, especially since they will need that kind of character to charge into the austere environments that we ask them to. With the dogs we train, we want and need each one to feel like he is "King of the World." We want the dogs to have a nasty, hard, confident attitude since they may very well be taking on insurgents who want nothing more than to kill them and their human associates. The dogs have got to want to charge through anything to go bite a guy who is trying to take them down.

I don't care how strong a dog is genetically. If he's been trained in that dominated, coercive, negative way, he's going to be much less capable than he could be. He will have learned that a human being can dominate him. Would you want to go into a friendly game of softball, let alone battle, thinking that? If you go into anything thinking you can get beat, chances are that is exactly what will happen.

7

PREP SCHOOL FOR PUPPIES

While some of the dogs I train come from abroad and may already be three years old when I acquire them, I also breed dogs right here and train their puppies so that, when they are mature, they are ready to work with a variety of governmental agencies or for private clients. In case there's any doubt, before we go any further, let me make it abundantly clear that for me—and for the puppies themselves—the beginning of the whole training process is more like fun than anything resembling work. Let me also make it clear that it *is* work I take seriously, because the training a dog gets during his very youngest days helps him grow to become a successful, mature working dog.

While what I do from the time a pup is born until he is ready for his advanced education may differ in some respects from what the SEAL team dogs go through in their first few days, weeks, and months in Europe, for all practical purposes, those differences are minor. We have the same goals: to maximize the natural abilities of the dogs; to identify their strengths and weaknesses; and to expose them to as many different things as possible so that they can more easily adapt to the specific circumstances they will encounter in their "careers."

The stages of training a SEAL dog or other working dog goes through are not unlike what the human members of the SEAL teams go through. Just like I did, every SEAL team member must first complete basic training and then one additional level of training before starting BUD/S training. The training puppies get, can be thought of as basic training.

It is interesting to note, however, that of those entering BUD/S training, 75 percent fail to complete the program. The failure rate is lower with SEAL dogs; approximately less than half don't make it through. I believe that part of the reason for this is that when I'm evaluating prospective team dogs, my standards are extremely high, and when I select dogs for breeding, I already know the kinds of work that their puppies will be asked to do once they've matured. So I can breed dogs with specific qualities they will pass on to their offspring that will help them learn what they need to.

Even before the puppies are born I try to optimize their chances of success by providing their mothers with the most stress-free environment possible while they are pregnant. Generally speaking, that means I move the mothers-to-be to a quieter part of the kennel, as far away as possible from the clamor of barking and other distractions. This also takes them out of any possible contact with aggressive or otherwise rambunctious dogs. At any one time, I may have as many as two dozen dogs around, including my own house pets. That many dogs can make a whole lot of noise. That's especially true because of the kind of kennel I've built for them. The kennel run has indoor/outdoor climate control and a septic system with heavy-duty drains. The kennel is all cinder block and coated with epoxy and is a cool and sturdy structure for the dogs to live in that allows them to be out of the weather. However, indoors the acoustics do not provide the most peaceful environment; the noise can be loud.

Several days after the puppies are born, their training begins. Every dog trainer has his or her own theories, and some of them are grounded in scientific research. A lot of them are not. They're either old wives' tales or just the experiences that a particular trainer has decided works best. The methods I use are based on lots of experience and research studies. I've had good results from using these training principles with puppies, and I've seen bad results when these methods aren't used.

Basically what it boils down to is this. Puppies are a kind of blank slate, but they absolutely retain some pack-animal instincts, which includes a tendency to be aggressive toward humans. However, as a species, dogs have been domesticated for centuries and are clearly adapted to living with people. Every dog has both these things hardwired into him. I believe that the amount of human interaction an individual dog gets from birth helps determine how that dog will be with people for its entire life. If they have very little human interaction in the first few months of their lives, they're going to be completely different than if they have a ton of human interaction. I give them a ton of human contact.

From when a puppy is three days old until he is twenty-one days old, we do something with him called "biosensor stressing." It sounds a lot more complicated than it is. Simply put, biosensor stressing is playing around with a puppy, but with a structured routine. When you pick the puppy up, you want to do a couple of things. One, you want to tickle his feet. Usually I'll take a Q-tip and stick it between a puppy's pads and his toes, making sure to stimulate each one of his paws. Along with that, I'll hold the puppy completely upright, with his head directly above his tail. I'll place him next to my face to let him smell me. I'll breathe on him, and I'll talk to him, too.

A puppy's sight, sense of smell, and hearing are not yet fully developed when he is born. That means, early on, neither my smell nor my physical presence is as fully recognizable to him as it will eventually be, but I want him to have that early sensory experience as soon as possible. That way, as the puppy is developing those senses more fully, he'll already have that early experience of what I smell like, what I sound like, and what I look like solidly in place. I want the dog to be comfortable with me. I also have multiple people do this so the puppy gets exposure to as many people as possible and therefore establishes a general comfort level with humans. I want a lot of different adults and children to be around puppies we're training. As you can probably figure out, it's not all that hard to get people to hold and play with puppies.

In the morning and at night I'll also usually take a cold, wet washcloth in my hand and set a puppy belly down on it for just a couple of seconds. Then I'll put him back in with the litter and take the next one out and do the same thing until I've done it with every one of them. Throughout the day I'll also constantly be picking up the puppies and just playing with them and holding them.

I also start to play CDs of random noises even though a puppy really doesn't hear much for the first three weeks of his life. Several different companies make these noise CDs that are typically used to expose police horses in training to a variety of different sounds. Essentially, these are "antispooking" noise CDs. They include train engines, whistles, firecrackers, thunder, machine guns, different farm animals, creaky doors, car and other engines, mufflers backfiring, sirens blaring, cars honking, and more. I play these CDs repeatedly to get the puppies accustomed to what is and will always be a very large part of their environment—sound.

Dogs have very sensitive hearing, and our selective breeding of them has enhanced that ability. Also, because of the structure of dogs' ears, they can hear sounds that are coming from a great distance. Pointed, erect ears are the most effective at capturing sound waves. Dogs can also hear sounds at higher frequencies than people can.

Anyone who has had a dog knows that certain sounds, such as the whine of a vacuum cleaner, can really irritate him. We play these CDs to such young puppies because, over the life of the dogs, we want them to have minimal, if any, reactions to unexpected sounds. We don't want to overstress the pups, but we do have to get them accustomed to hearing a variety of noises at various volumes. Later, when we do helicopter training with the K-9 candidates, that early exposure to sounds almost always pays off. All you can ever do in training is simulate how the real world of the dogs' working lives will be. There is, of course, no guarantee to how any given dog will respond in those real-world circumstances. Training is all about enhancing the likelihood of a good outcome down the road. According to a study conducted by the U.S. military, mildly stressing puppies helps their immune systems develop and helps them mature more quickly.

— • —

At about the time the pups are weaned I'll stop using the noise CDs and shift into another phase of their early training. At this point, I begin to work on evaluating and enhancing their prey drive. To do that, I'll take a rag, something like a terry cloth dish towel, and tease a pup with it. I want the pup to get his eyes focused on it so he chases it. I'll tease the pup a little bit. He chases, chases, chases. Then, *bam*! I reward the pup by letting him get the rag. We play a little bit of tug, and then I reward him again by letting him have the rag. The pup chews on the rag, which is basically a dog instinctively tearing his prey apart.

One of the other things I do is wean the dogs early. Some people wait until puppies are seven or eight weeks old to start weaning them from their mother. I wean them at about four weeks. I do this for two reasons. One, it's a lot easier on the mother. Two, I want a lot more human interaction at this point. I want to allow the puppies to get some of their mannerisms and character from their mom, but I need to be present to teach them some manners— not to mention a ton of other things.

The single most important aspect of a dog's training for the work they do is to establish a bond of trust between handler and dog. That begins in those very early days when we first start the work to get the puppies accustomed to human contact. If the pups are left with their littermates, and they have no or limited human interaction, they're going to be very, very pack oriented, or very, very animal dependent. On the flip side, dogs raised this way are going to be much weaker when they are eventually separated from their litter, their pack. So I try to get an individual pup with me and around other people as early as possible because that's the environment the dog is going to be in for the rest of his life. He's going to be paired up with a human, like Chopper was with Brett in the SEALs. The dogs are going to be in kennels and crates and thrust into different environments, doing different kinds of work. So, from day one, I begin to get it ingrained in them that this is the standard, this is the routine, and then that becomes what they know as their "normal" and what they are comfortable with. It makes it much easier for them in the long run and prevents them from being confused by and potentially freezing up in any kind of new situation.

If you think about it, the same is true with people. New environments and new things in those environments can cause us to not perform at our best. The navy has known this for a long time. That's why they place such an importance on training exercises. The closer a simulation can be to the real thing, the better prepared the troops will be. This may seem obvious, but it's worth pointing out that all the simulation work makes members of the navy—both human and canine—more able to focus completely on the mission when they are deployed.

Again, because adaptability to an environment is so key to a working dog's success, I do a couple of other things to enhance both the pups' prey drive and their comfort level with the unfamiliar. Even at that age I start taking them all over the place. We go to the local hospital, to playgrounds, to Home Depot, you name it. Since the dogs will be transported to various locations a lot during training and afterward, getting them used to being in vehicles is an essential component. We also want to expose each of the pups to people in different circumstances, be it people in wheelchairs or on crutches or kids sitting in shopping carts. We go into parking lots and let tons of people handle and play with them. We take the pups on escalators and elevators and expose them to loud noises, dark rooms, and slippery floors. As soon as I can get these dogs exposed to stuff like that, I do it.

I also do the rag work in all these different types of environments. I'll even set up a little puppy obstacle course. Basically, I put all sorts of different objects and obstacles in their path. This includes lengths of PVC pipe lying on the ground or a little baby pool filled with plastic bottles and a hidden toy or ball. I take the pups to a suspension bridge that's elevated and wobbly and get them around fence grating and multileveled pallets. I want them to have to crawl up and over things, to go underground at times, and to be familiar with and comfortable in all kinds of terrain. One of my favorite sights is the dogs diving into that kiddy pool filled with empty plastic bottles in pursuit of that ball or toy. Later, when the pups get bigger, I do this on a larger scale with an old bathtub filled with plastic balls. This looks a lot like those pits of balls that some indoor playgrounds have for younger kids, but while some little kids might hesitate before stepping into one of those pits, it's a rare dog that will pause on the edge of a pool or tub to think about it before diving in.

I really enjoy working with the pups at all stages, but I do get a big kick out of the obstacle course. It essentially is a doggy Disneyland for the pups, and it's great to watch them figure out all the "rides." That doesn't mean that my interaction with them is limited to watching. At this stage, I'm very much into hands-on play with them. That includes me throwing a lot of mini tennis balls and other toys. I also still do a lot of rag work and tug-of-war with tug balls attached to a string. I yank on the string to get that tug ball moving, which keeps the pups in pursuit of something—using their prey drive—as much as possible. I also really want these dogs to develop their sense of possession—that there's something out there they have to get, and once they do it belongs to them. Later on, we'll work more intently on the letting-go part, but at this stage we really feed their desire to chase and catch things.

To reinforce the idea that these other locations are pleasurable and that actually being in them is some kind of reward, I will also feed the pups. Of course each individual Malinois pup's food drive is a bit unique, as it is with any breed of dog. Even so, any reward experience a pup has that pairs the environment or place he is in with the receiving of a reward or meeting of a need is positive reinforcement.

I also start to feed the pups to get them used to using their noses early on. While they are still with their mom, I'll take a bowl of food and set it somewhere in the room. Not right out in the middle, but somewhere they have to search for it a bit. You'll very quickly see the pups catch the scent and start using their noses to go find it. After a few days of that, I put the food in another room, somewhere just beyond the door to the room they are in. Now they come into the other room and the same thing happens. The pups get wind of the food, and they all use their noses to find that bowl.

Every couple of days I'll up the ante, so to speak, and make it more challenging for them. Next we'll go outside to a field that is 270 to 330 square feet. At first I put them down very near where I've hidden the food, because I want to set them up for success, and a young pup's attention span is incredibly short. As time goes on, I'll hide the food in the deep weeds farther away. Then I'll hide it several acres away, and they'll just start walking toward it. It's important to understand that I'm not trying to frustrate them. I just want them to earn their taste of success. That's why when I go out to hide the food, I always place it somewhere downwind so that when they first step outside, they'll pick up the food's scent pretty quickly. Then, as soon as they do catch a whiff of it, they go charging out toward it.

By doing things this way, I'm actually working with the pups on several things all at once. First, I've taught them to use their noses and to be successful at it. They have gotten repeated, positive results at an early age, and that helps teach them to trust and rely on their sense of smell.

They've also had to do some work, though. When we're out in a large area, they have to stick with it and keep air-scenting and walking along with me. We'll walk and we'll walk, and then *bam*! All of a sudden the pups are into the odor and they go into locate-the-source mode. This is exactly what they're going to be doing if they do detection work later on.

When doing detection work, a dog will take as many as ten short breaths a second to move scents far into his nasal cavity. Imagine a human trying to cover the distances these dogs do, going for miles at a time, while employing that kind of breathing pattern. We'd likely faint before we'd finish. While dogs, particularly herding dogs like the Malinois, naturally have strong endurance capabilities, that trait also has to be carefully nurtured and developed. Eventually the pups that grow up to do detection work will travel great distances on walks, sometimes while wearing weighted vests.

If it sounds like I'm being pretty demanding on these pups at an early age, I am. It's because these dogs are being trained to be working dogs. I know what their role in life is going to be, so I know the kinds of skills they are going to need to be successful. If you look at people who are successful at a sport, for example, chances are good that they began *playing* (note the emphasis here) their chosen sport at a very early age. The best athletes are generally the ones who picked up their game very early on in life. Sure, you could become a pro golfer, tennis player, baseball player, or whatever if you started at the age of fifteen, but the odds are against you. The earlier you start, the better your chances of being at the top of your sport someday.

From birth to eighteen months, a dog goes through a rapid period of mental and physical growth. It grows from a helpless infant into an animal possessing the vast majority of its adult capabilities. It's my job to help each dog maximize his abilities.

Just so it's clear, no puppy has starved or been injured in any way during the early training phase. I'm never punishing the pups in any way. Instead, I'm teaching them, from an early age, to work for a reward. In a lot of respects, as serious as the training business is, those pups are having a blast.

8

DETECTION TRAINING:
PASSING THE SNIFF TEST

I squatted against the wall in the dark, breathing the moist air, hiding from the dogs working the detection-training exercise. I was waiting for them to detect me, to pick up my scent with their noses and come find me. I don't know if words can adequately describe the feelings of anticipation and dread that you experience when you're in a situation like that, knowing that any second, a 60- to 80-pound monster is going to steamroll you. It is more than sweaty-palms time, let me tell you, but the thrill of it never gets old.

Because of how complex the situation was that I had set up for the dogs, I was confident that I had plenty of time before any of them detected me.

I was wrong.

Within minutes, the first dog came blasting out of the darkness to pound into me. Even though I was wearing a protective bite suit, I walked off that field of battle with sore and rapidly swelling forearms, hands, and legs. Another trainer named Wayne and I switched on and off being the decoy all day, and we lost every time to the dogs. The dogs and their handlers did a stellar job that day. So my body may have taken a few hits, but my pride at seeing the dogs excel at their training wasn't wounded in the least.

— —

On that training day we were in a compound we had access to that was spread out over two or three acres in the foothills of some local mountains. There were eight buildings scattered across the compound. Given the nature of today's warfare and the kinds of battlegrounds on which wars are played out, we have to simulate not only mountainous terrain for the dogs but urban environments, too. Building searches are a common part of a MWD's duties.

We had six dogs and six handlers working that day. There were three similar buildings on the compound, each like what you might find at boot camp. Each building had about a hundred two-tiered beds, a couple of common-area rooms, a large mess/kitchen area, some storage rooms, and, most critical to this exercise, two larger shower areas and bathrooms. In other words, these were sprawling buildings with multiple good hiding spots.

We picked the largest of the buildings for our hiding spot. I explained the training exercise to the handlers by saying, "Okay, you guys are going to patrol in, cordon off security, and go into this building and try to find a high-value target in there." That means the handlers and the dogs were going to make their way into the compound and secure it. Then they were going to enter the largest building and look for the high-value target. That target would be me in a bite suit.

I thought the scenario I set up would trip up the dogs because of the combination of elements they would encounter. This was a daytime exercise, but I blacked out all the windows, so it was dark in there. A dog's vision isn't as negatively affected as ours is when we go from a bright room to a pitch-black one, but, like us, a dog still needs some adjustment time. I selected a hiding spot in the shower area that was as far from the building's entry point as possible. To add to the confusion caused by the dark, I turned on all the showerheads with the water running full blast. In my mind this was going to be a major obstacle, the equivalent of a dog working his way through an outdoor waterfall in the middle of the night.

My intention to make it tougher on the dog by having the water running turned into a serious disadvantage not for the dog but for me. I was in a huge bite suit, wrestling with a wet dog. It was all I could do to keep my footing on the slippery tile floor while I waited for the dog's handler to find me and get the dog off me. I didn't need it, but there it was anyway: more proof that I had trained this dog well, because at this point in his training, which was about nineteen months in, he only obeyed the handler he was teamed with—and that was as it should be.

— —

The object of detection-work training is to take full advantage of a dog's innate ability to detect odors far better than a human can. As also mentioned earlier, a dog has, on average, 220 million scent receptors. A person has about 5 million. In 1999, researchers at Auburn University's Institute for Biological Detection Systems conducted experiments on dogs' scent receptors to better understand how they worked. They also conducted specific studies to see how little of an odor of something need be present in order for a dog to detect it. The study found that dogs could detect various explosives when only an extraordinarily small amount of the chemicals was present. They were also able to detect tiny amounts of other chemical "tags" that are used in explosives. Many governments, including our own, require odorous chemical tags to be placed in explosives as identifiers. That gives us some extra options with dogs that do detection work. In case a dog is not able to detect the explosives themselves, maybe he can detect those "taggant" chemicals instead. Either way, when a dog is trained to pick up the scent of explosives, you know when he's found them because he is trained to give a physical response when he does, like that marine detection dog in Tikrit, Iraq, who sat down, his ears pointed straight up, when he came to the explosive-rigged hut.

Another thing the Auburn study mentioned was that it's not

the amount of a hidden explosive that is important with a dog doing detection work. Instead, what's important is distance. The farther a dog is from where the explosives are hidden, the fewer molecules of odor are available. This may seem obvious, but because of a dog's keen sensitivity to odors, he will hit on that small number of molecules and know which way to go because the concentration of odor molecules increases as the dog nears the hidden explosives. Any object gives off an "odor cone" like that—molecules of odor travel out and away from the source. A dog's ability to detect odors allows him, once trained, to lock in on that odor cone and follow it.

— • —

Dogs who are trained to be multipurpose working dogs will spend the majority of their time detecting odors while working in the field. Detection work is very complicated, and a large part of a dog's specialized training time is spent on developing the skills to detect multiple odors.

You might be wondering: How do you really train a dog to detect something, whether it's a person, an explosive, or anything else? Exposure to the target scent and an association with it come into play again here, as does repetition. This is how dogs (and people) learn: through association and repetition. Dogs especially need routine; it's how they live their lives. So, detection training is extremely time consuming because it requires a trainer to follow a lot of structured and precise steps. There are as many as two hundred steps to doing detection work well. As I work with a dog and we progress through those steps, if we encounter any snags along the way, we'll fall back a few steps and then work forward again. Hopefully we move past the problem area and on to the next exacting part of the training process. A dog will have performed some of these detection exercises and tasks thousands of times before being deployed.

However, it's a different story when it comes to detecting explosives. In my experience, with explosives you don't need thousands of repetitions to get dogs to recognize a specific chemical signature for something like TNT. It takes them only a handful of times to become familiar with the scent and be able to detect it. For a dog, TNT has a very distinct and memorable scent. To some degree, it's no different from you being able to positively identify the odor of something like skunk without having had a lot of repeated exposure to it. How many times did you need to smell skunk before you knew what it was?

Trainers use a lot of different methods when they work with a dog on initial exposure to and detection of explosives. The one I use I refer to simply as retrieving.

The obvious point about explosive-odor detection is that you have to introduce the dogs to that chemical signature safely somehow. The thing you use to expose the dog to that odor is essentially irrelevant. You can use anything that will retain that small bit of explosive material. For example, you can drill holes in a piece of PVC pipe and enclose the chemical in that, or you can put it in a box or on a towel. I use rags, bits of terry cloth towel, and I'm extremely careful with how I use them—not because they could explode but because they can become easily contaminated. I wear extrathick gloves whenever I'm handling the samples to avoid my odor signature from getting mixed in with the explosive scent. I'll place several pounds of explosives, which is considered a small amount, in a plastic box along with a quantity of towels. After about a month, the explosive odor will have worked its way into the fabric. At that point, I can then separate the towels and seal them individually in an airtight container. Needless to say, I label that container.

Early in the exposure regimen to imprint an odor on a dog, I won't be too concerned about the environment in which we do the work. That will come later. Once I have rags that are ready, I take a dog out, along with his handler, and we work on the simplest level. I throw the towel, and the dog retrieves it. His reward, when he brings the rag back to his handler, is that he gets to play tug for a little bit with the towel. We repeat this fifteen or so times, and by the end, the dog is familiar with that odor. I use a new towel each time to make certain that the dog is fixed on that odor and not on the combination of dirt, grass, spit, the handler's odor, or anything else. It takes the dog all of about ten minutes to become imprinted on the odor, far less time than it takes me to do all the prep work.

After the imprinting, we move on to what's called point-to-point exercises. For this, I need a fenced-off area. A ball field works really well. I take a sample of an explosive chemical odor and put it on the backside and upwind side of the fence. I may place about half a pound of a selected target odor there. I then take the dog, or have the handler take his dog, and I give the search command, very often using the Dutch word "*Szook*." Then I walk alongside that fence so that we are parallel to the chain link, downwind and in a straight line. Depending upon how hard the wind is blowing, we may start out walking toward the dynamite from only about 15 feet away. The wind blowing across that dynamite picks up the odor cone. It starts out narrow and concentrated at the source and then widens. Picture the beam of a flashlight.

As we're walking and entering that odor cone, I'm watching the dog to see any change in his behavior. When a dog hits on the odor, his head will snap in the odor's direction, his tail will feather or twitch, and he will move in the direction of the source. He'll get up to the fence but not actually be able to touch the explosive, lick it, or eat it. At that point, I issue either a sit or a down command for the dog, which will serve as the alert to let the handler know, "Here it is." The dog does that, I hit the clicker, and then he gets his reward.

We work through that scenario one odor at a time over and over until we move through all the possible detection scenarios for all the desired target odors we want to teach a dog to recognize. An advantage I have as a former SEAL is that I understand and have experience with the tactical side of explosives, with the way they're used. I can create more realistic scenarios for the dogs to work in than someone who is a dog trainer first and an explosive-detection dog trainer second. I was trained as a SEAL, I was deployed as a SEAL, I've trained SEAL team members, and now I use all that to train MWDs to assist SEAL teams. Having been there and done all that means that I can be as precise as possible, giving these incredibly talented animals the benefit of all my experience.

To get a dog to detect anything, not just explosives, you basically follow the same fundamental principles and steps: initial exposure to and imprinting of the scent, followed by point-to-point exercises, followed by placing the object in various environmental scenarios.

In order for a dog to function effectively in any of those environmental scenarios, such as the one I created in the compound, he has to be physically fit. So detection (and other) training includes taking a dog on runs and taking him swimming, then having the dog do these things with his handler. A dog also does resistance training. This can be done with weights, where the dog wears a harness and drags weights attached to it. Or it can be done with bungee cord leashes, which produce greater resistance the farther they are extended. The entire dog gets a workout and gets into top physical shape—from nose to tail.

9

APPREHENSION TRAINING:
SINKING THEIR TEETH INTO IT

Arras and his handler, Matt, were out on night patrol, making their way across a steep mountain with its jagged rocks. Suddenly a figure appeared and in quick succession shot off a couple of rounds of gunfire before running off. Matt gave Arras a command, and without hesitation the dog bolted into the darkness. Within minutes Arras located and subdued the shooter, tackling him to the ground.

The shooter was actually a "decoy," a trainer in a bite suit, and Arras and Matt were participating in a nighttime apprehension-training exercise with gunfire. Arras had performed the apprehension part well, and when Matt issued the "out" command he backed off and left the shooter. However, the dog was still very green in his training. So when he left one man in a bite suit on the ground and turned and faced Matt, he could not see his handler's face. Matt's face was obscured by the huge night operational device, or night-vision goggles, he had on so he could see in the dark. Arras was still feeling the aggression he had used to apprehend the shooter. So instead of Matt he thought he saw someone he didn't know, someone who, like the man he had just apprehended, was also carrying a gun. Arras responded by taking off after Matt. He leapt up on him and bit him in the middle of the chest. He drove Matt to the ground, where he had him in a very vulnerable position. Thankfully, he realized through Matt's scent and a few other triggers that this was not the enemy. This was Matt, the guy who took good care of him, and he released him immediately.

— -

Apprehension work clearly incorporates detection work—first, Arras had to find the shooter—but apprehension work is primarily about one thing, bite work. Arras had to find the decoy in order to bite him. Biting him was Arras's reward. In detection training and work, dogs are known to get very excited when they hear the search word command *"Szook,"* but the search word command *"Reviere,"* which is used in apprehension training and work, makes dogs go positively nuts. It is as if every cell in their bodies and every bit of their canine ancestry are turned on. The dogs know they are going to detect and apprehend a person. They know that they are going to be able to do what is probably their favorite thing of all—bite someone.

During apprehension training, we frequently use the mountains at night, because that combination produces about the most difficult environment the dogs and their handlers will encounter. As they both grow more confident and competent in their training, we up the ante. The dogs and handlers have to be prepared to deal with the possibility of enemy contact and engagement when deployed. That means they will encounter, and have to react to, weapons.

By the time we introduce nighttime gunfire into a mountain exercise, a dog, like Arras, has already been exposed to the sound of weapons being fired. Essentially, these dogs have been hardwired through breeding and training to have an aggressive response to the sound of a weapon's discharge. They associate the sound of gunfire with aggression. That's both good and bad. A dog could be on a mission in which there is constant gunfire. In an instance like that, an immediate aggressive response to gunfire would not be sound. Consequently, part of our work is to get them to *not* respond to gunfire. We desensitize them to the sound and teach them to only go into apprehension mode on command. The only way to do that is to fire round after round near them, reward them when they don't freak out, and restrain them when they do.

In a fast-moving, dark, and chaotic scenario like the one Arras and Matt experienced, it's easy to understand why Arras, at that point in his training, responded the way he did. His aggression level and desire to bite someone were on full boil, and it was hard for him, at this point, to turn it down to a simmer. It's also easy to understand why we were all so grateful that he didn't utilize his full capabilities as a biter on Matt. Anyone involved in the training of these dogs has to have, or will quickly develop, respect for the potential threat that these dogs pose.

Many studies have been conducted over the years to determine the bite force of dogs and a variety of other animals. In 2005, as part of a National Geographic Television series, Dr. Brady Barr equipped a bite sleeve with a computerized measuring instrument to test the biting strength of people and several other species. His human test subjects reached 127 pounds of pressure, while domestic dogs averaged 320 pounds. This means that the average dog's bite is close to being three times as strong as that of a person. Impressive as that sounds and *is*, think about this. Lions and white sharks can exert 600 pounds of biting pressure. Just to keep that in perspective, hyenas can exert 1,000 pounds of pressure when they bite. The champ, though, is the crocodile, which in Dr. Barr's test reached 6,000 pounds of biting force. Clearly, it's a good thing that most of us will never find ourselves in a situation with a lion, white shark, hyena, or crocodile. However, we are all pretty much in the vicinity of one dog or another at some point in our lives. As I said, you have to respect the potential force of a dog's jaws.

The University of Guelph in Ontario, Canada, conducted a study that actually analyzed dogs' jaws and jaw muscles. The study concluded that a Malinois can bite with around 160 pounds of force with the teeth at the front of its jaw and with a gripping 550 pounds of force with its molars at the rear of its jaw. That the back of the mouth has the ability to exert a greater force makes sense, if you think about it. The back of the mouth is closer to the "lever," or hinge, of the jaw, where the upper and lower halves of the jaw meet. In fact, if you ever observed your dog when you play tug with him, you probably noticed pretty quickly that the dog understands something about the physics of bite force, because he works pretty hard to get whatever he has between his teeth into the back of his mouth in order to hold on to it more securely. If you've ever attempted to pull a tennis ball out of your dog's mouth, you know that it's easier if the ball is at the front of your dog's mouth and not the back. Check this out next time you're playing with a dog.

It's also pretty obvious that a dog will first bite with the front of his mouth; after all, that's the widest opening and has the easiest access to things. You can go on the Internet and see videos of protection dogs and other working dogs doing bite work, and you'll see some pretty spectacular flashing of jaws and snarling and men in bite suits getting these dogs to grab and hold on with those front-of-jaw bites. It all looks great, but as you know now, those bites won't exert as much force as when the back of the jaw clamps down. Those canine teeth are sharp, and they will puncture skin, but when it comes to bone-crushing power, and the ability to really hold on to and subdue an adversary, a dog will have to get his back teeth on someone.

Similarly, you can also see amazing scenes of dogs flying up, all four paws off the ground, to go after trainers in bite suits. These dogs launch themselves from 20 feet away and then contact their targets. Again, it all looks great. It's just not very effective. As any football coach will tell you, don't leave your feet. Why?

As a former football player, I can tell you that it's hard to change direction in midair. As a dog trainer who's been in various apprehension/bite training scenarios, I know you can't change direction very easily when your feet are off the ground. It's also easier to move to the left or right (when you do have your feet on the floor) and avoid a charging dog, especially one that doesn't have four (or even two) feet on the floor. In addition, the amount of force and leverage you lose when you're airborne, as opposed to when your feet are solidly planted on the planet, is substantial. In the National Football League, for instance, a soaring tackle against the guy carrying the ball may make the highlights reel, but it's the tackle that happens when the defensive player is firmly planted on the ground that is not just more fundamentally sound but can also be a harder hit.

As far as the dogs are concerned, those leaps are also potentially dangerous to the dog's well-being. For example, if a dog is chasing after someone on a roof and the dog sails off the roof in pursuit, he could hit a wall or otherwise do some serious damage to himself.

As for serious damage, let me tell you that even with a bite suit on—and that's a specially padded suit designed to absorb a lot of the force of an animal's jaws—I have felt the power of a dog's body and jaws, and that is not something to take lightly. I have at times when wearing this protective gear experienced a level of pain as intense as anything I've endured in my entire life.

I have also, in fact, been on the receiving end of a dog's bites and blows without having any protective gear on. That is an incredibly humbling experience. Let me tell you, all studies and analysis aside, when a dog gets his maximum bite force on me, it is incredible. The pain is sharp and intense, my vision narrows, sounds seem to be silenced, and thoughts of how I can mess with this dog and get the better of him are replaced by a single thought— *I wish this dog would just get off of me.*

—◆—

I need to make this point clear. The apprehension work that we do with the dogs is to train them as a *nonlethal* force. In most cases, a live capture of a suspected, or clearly demonstrated insurgent, Taliban member, or whatever bad guy the dog goes after is much preferred over a "neutralized" one. A lot of valuable intelligence information has been and can be extracted from captured combatants. That is one of the reasons why I consider dogs to be such an effective weapon—they are trained to be a very highly skilled nonlethal force, trained to exert, yet restrain, their biting force.

Actually, all those numbers about bite force pale in comparison to something that's much more difficult to quantify—and that is the measure of a dog's heart and how much a dog is willing to endure in order to subdue a human being. How many of them are willing to use that biting force at the expense of their own discomfort? That's what the initial bite-work training in a contained area like the apprehension-training corral we set up is all about and focuses on. Think about it like this. We work on developing a dog's tenacity in close combat, similar to the way a boxer spars in the ring. We're also working to develop each dog's technique, but it's also about getting each dog to utilize his inherent aggression and push past a pain boundary. There may be some physical pain, but I'm mostly referring to mental stress. It's the mental stress a dog undergoes when he feels you fighting back, when he feels your own mental and emotional aggression working against his forces; it's when the two of you are really locked in combat and you are testing the dog's willingness to get the job done.

Working in a bite suit against a dog is as much an acting job as it is a physical performance. Similar to what the dogs have to endure, more than just your physical stamina is being tested. As I said earlier, dogs read body language, and they also read the energetic projections you give off. If you are working with a dog on his apprehension and bite skills, you have to be mentally strong and able to project the same kind of "I'm bigger and badder than you" attitude. Anyone can go through the motions of standing there in a padded suit while a dog grabs you; it takes a good bit of artistry to act the part (and believe me, it isn't completely acting) of someone who has deadly intent. Dogs are highly sensitive to those signals we humans send out, and when we're afraid they absolutely get it and take full advantage of it. It's how they respond when you match aggression for aggression that determines whether or not they will make the cut with us.

Just to give you a sense of how strongly dogs respond to signals we send out, I have a close friend, Wayne, who can give off a fierce "don't mess with me" vibe even when he's lying on the ground, which is a very compromising position to be in with these dogs. When we release a dog to come after him, the dog will tear out initially and then come skidding to a stop six feet in front of Wayne, sensing that "this is one bad dude and I better be careful." Wayne is a former Navy Search and Rescue Corpsman, and he's taught me a lot about dogs and is one of the real friends I've got in this life. I've got plenty of buddies, but just a few friends, and Wayne is one of them. We frequently work together in training MWDs, and Wayne brings a wealth of experience and insight into the mix, along with his "don't mess with me" attitude that the dogs sense. Wayne doesn't shout. He doesn't strike any offensive postures. He just exudes that attitude, and the dogs feel it and respond accordingly.

The way that we get dogs to match aggression for aggression is by shifting them between drives. When you're doing apprehension or bite work, there are two main drives that a dog is working. He's working in prey drive, or on the offensive, and he's also working his defensive drive. In bite work, a dog starts out in prey drive, and that's very instinctual.

The dog sees a guy in a bite suit, he gets the command, and *bam*! The dog goes after the guy. The dog is conditioned to fight with the guy. What usually happens in much of the bite-work training other dogs receive is that they aren't truly put into defensive-drive mode. I equate that to a boxer who's been taught how to box but has never been hit. So you've got to teach this dog how to get hit, how to react. You can teach anybody how to throw punches all night long, how to move around the ring and counterpunch, but if they've never actually been hit, the first time they are, they're like, what was that? So you've got to teach that dog that, hey, not only is it okay, but you're going to work through it.

It's a very, very simple but not easy process. You've got to have a truckload of experience with seeing dogs being worked and then also working with them to really be able to identify each of the two drives and know how and when to shift a dog from one drive into the other and then back and forth again and again. Prey drive relieves a dog's stress. A dog feels like this is the natural order of things. He's thinking, "I'm being the aggressor. I'm taking my aggression to that thing/that person. I'm going to dominate it."

When in prey drive, a dog detects something and his mouth is on it. He's biting down, he's scoring the touchdown. He's going after it. He's loving life. Then, all of a sudden, the decoy in the bite suit comes alive and starts bringing it to him. This turns the whole process around for the dog. Now the dog is thinking, "Now I'm going to fight. Now I'm going on defense. Now I'm getting a little bit worried about this guy. I'm fighting him a little harder, maybe a third round, whatever." You've got to be able to recognize when a dog is on offense and when a dog is on defense. Put a dog too much on the defensive and for too long, and he will crack—and we can't have that happen.

To keep the dog on the aggressive, we gradually increase those defensive thresholds by shifting the dog back and forth between prey drive and defensive drive, so he's thinking, "I'm going after it. I'm preserving my life." Over time, that threshold for defense goes up and up and up, enough to where now that dog is automatically coming at you like he wants to kill you. It doesn't matter what you do to him, he is completely unfazed by it. It may start out with the dog in prey drive. You start to put a little bit of pressure on him so he switches into defense drive, and he starts to wig out a little bit. *Bam!* You switch things right back so the dog goes into prey drive and can relieve that stress. Now you put the dog back into defense drive. Now he lasts a few seconds longer. When he starts to show stress again, *bam*. Every time he starts to get to that boiling point, *bam*, you get him right back into prey drive. I back off, I reward him, I look away from him, I let him dominate me, and I take a bite to the back. Maybe I even fall to the ground and let him really dominate me.

It's a feeling-out process that you have to be constantly evaluating as you go. A truly good decoy is absolutely priceless because he will make or break a dog. You can ruin a great dog with an incompetent decoy, or make an average dog fantastic by having a phenomenal decoy who can recognize when to shift drives and know how much pressure to put on, when to back off, when to relieve stress, and when to put it on.

In my mind, doing this kind of bite work is absolutely an art. You have to eventually develop a feel for how stressed an individual dog gets, recognize his body language and how he is communicating, and understand what he is thinking and feeling, before you can really train a dog well. You need to elevate a dog to a level where you're teaching him how to fight, how to bring up that natural instinct that he has genetically deep down, an instinct that we've already identified through the training-selection process. Now we're just teaching him to bring that genetic instinct up to a much higher level, so he is able to handle the rigors of training. Eventually we arrive at the dog being ten times the dog he was when we first got him.

Like other aspects of training MWDs, this is a time-consuming process. If you're not careful, you can create a couple of problems. One is that if you don't put the dog into defensive drive enough, he never really learns how to fight. This is certainly better than burning him out going the other way, which is putting him on the defensive too much. That way you've cracked and ruined the dog and broken his spirit, so that he relinquishes a lot of the backbone that he had. As a result, we always err on the side of prey drive and don't take the dogs overboard on defense drive.

Unless you've seen these dogs in action, it's difficult to convey the differences in their responses when in each of the two drives. It is a matter of degree of intensity as well as specific behaviors. In terms of intensity, think of your dog when you reward him with a treat—he takes it readily and willingly but is gentle and nonaggressive. When you give your dog a treat and other dogs are present, your dog's sense of competition for resources is higher. He will take the treat, reaching for it more aggressively; in some cases, a dog will turn his head and his eyes seem to roll back in the same way that a great white shark does when attacking prey. Your dog won't bite you in order to get the treat, but he is definitely amped up a notch or two. That's how it is when an MWD shifts from one drive to the other. Because the intensity is already well beyond your treat-seeking dog's drive, his amped-up behavior feels that much more aggressive/assertive/on the offensive.

— —

A dog that will only fight when in a kind of training corral isn't any good to us or to anyone who wants a dog trained to do apprehension work. Neither is a dog that can be distracted by other things that may be happening around him. So another important component of apprehension training is to place a dog into a variety of environments at the appropriate time, just like we do with detection training. We travel far and wide with a dog and his handler and create a variety of scenarios so that each dog has the experience of tracking and apprehending bad guys in everything from mountainous terrain at night to urban settings both indoors and outdoors.

One new environment for the dogs is a helicopter. We work with them on a similar kind of exposure work to the aircraft. It starts with just having the dogs be around a helicopter and progresses to them getting into one and then to actually taking off and landing in one. After that we get the dogs to fly in a helicopter for greater and greater distances. We refer to the taking-off and landing exercises as elevators. We place one dog in each helicopter along with a complement of a flight crew and a team. The dog and handler are the last to board. We do the full load-up of the aircraft, and then the dog and handler get on. We take off and then land two to three minutes later, repeating this process six to eight times with each dog.

Everyone knows that a dog just starting out with this training can be a bit uneasy, and I've watched people on board press themselves as far back against the sides of the chopper as they can when the handler and the dog board, hoping to stay out of an unsettled dog's way and not attract his attention. Once, we had a relatively inexperienced flyer doing elevators. Everyone else in the cabin was a handler, so they knew what to look for, and they all watched the dog and immediately wallpapered themselves. They could see the dog defaulting to aggression mode, and he eyed each and every one of them, assessing who would be the choicest bite. The men kept pressing themselves against the wall, trying to make themselves as small a target as possible. I had to laugh a bit when I saw that. Five combat-trained and hardened military men—all heavily armed, mind you—trying to keep as far away as they could from this pacing menace. Obviously, part of our job is to get the dogs to calm down and not pose such a threat, but those exercises serve as a good reminder to all of us about just what kind of power these dogs really have over us and how we have to do everything we can to harness it and unleash it properly.

I think it bears repeating that you can't make a dog get over reverting to his aggression mode by doing anything punitive to him. You run the risk of inciting him even more and increasing his aggressive response. Then you have to be even more punitive, and eventually you absolutely break the dog's spirit. What we try to do is make those frightening and unfamiliar experiences, like being around and in a helicopter for the first time, more pleasant through the use of rewards. In training, whether it's bite work or getting a dog used to a muzzle or anything else, I always carry some treats with me. By treats I mostly mean toys or food rewards. When I'm working, I carry both. I even take soft treats and mash them against the inside of a muzzle cage to get dogs who are unwilling to put their snouts in there to get them to associate the muzzle with something they like, something positive. At first, just letting them eat treats out of it is an effective way to get them used to the sight of the muzzle. When it comes time to place the muzzle over the dog's head and snout, it's a much easier thing to accomplish if he isn't already on high alert and anxiety at the sight of the thing.

No matter what you're trying to do with a dog to train him for the role he will play in combat or in your life, it's important that he believes some positive reward is coming his way. As trainers and handlers, our positive-reward system also provides us with a growing confidence that we won't be the ones a dog turns his considerable bite force on.

➤ ━

How exactly do we refine a dog's innate skills to make him effective at apprehending individuals? Just as with detection work, we start a dog early and continually increase the complexity and duration of the exercises—moving the dog from play as a pup to more serious work as he becomes an adult. We push each dog to near his breaking point.

Beginning when a pup is four to five weeks old, we start to develop and encourage his prey instinct. We always take advantage of a dog's inherent desire to want to chase moving objects. So we'll take a terry cloth towel or a rag, something that's very easy for the pup to grip, and something we can tease him with easily. We'll begin the process of developing the dog's prey instinct so that it becomes a useful skill for things other than just playing tug-of-war.

As you've probably experienced if you've ever raised a pup, when you wave something in front of him he's going to chase after it and try to grab it. In our work, we do something similar, but with the intent to get a pup frustrated that we're the ones that have hold of the rag. We play a little tug with him, and then when he bites in deeper we give him counterpressure by pulling back slightly. Then we hold still. The dog will usually naturally pull and then counter and go a little deeper. When he does that, I'll let go and reward him by letting him have the towel or rag. It's as if I'm saying, *Okay, you chased it, caught it, killed it, now you get to carry your prey off and prance around with it. It's yours and you get to have it. Have fun.*

From there, we advance to doing that work in all different types of environments. We do it in buildings, out in fields, in dark places, inside vehicles, or anywhere else that a pup may or may not be during his later training or when he's downrange. A pup is not just environmentally going places. He's chasing balls in those environments. He's doing rag and bite work in those environments.

Just as in every other step of dog training, over time, we take very small and slow baby steps forward. From rags we progress to a puppy sleeve, which is basically a jute pillow. Jute is a pretty coarse fabric, but it's very soft and very easy for a dog to grab onto. Then we apply the same principles we used with the rags and terry cloth towels.

Sometimes we'll take an empty 20-ounce plastic bottle, flatten it, tie it to a string, and tie the string to a pole. Then we'll "flirt pole" the dog with that and tease him with it. It's a tease because it's

— · —

I have to admit that as serious as this work is for me, I take a lot of pleasure in creating and participating in these on-site exercises. Just thinking about driving along in an ATV at 35 to 40 miles per hour up a mountain pass where we do a lot of the training, with the dogs keeping up with us for 800 yards of elevation gain for about three-quarters of a mile, gives me an added appreciation for these dogs. They lope along in that classic herder stride, a combination of seemingly effortless athletic grace and fierce determination that gets my heart pumping every time with awe and pride.

— · —

As I mentioned earlier, a dog can be seriously injured, or even killed, if he is turned loose to apprehend someone on a roof or if he is fighting someone who can grab and hurt his legs. This is also true if he is turned loose to apprehend someone who is near a window. During training, as a safety precaution, the dogs are kept on leashes during some of the exercises. Whether a dog is kept on a leash or not when he's in the field will depend on the actual situation he is in. His handler will have to make the decision about when to release the dog, and it generally has to do with when a dog shows a sign that he has picked up the scent trail of a human. So, during these training exercises for apprehension, one of the things I do is evaluate each handler's decisions. I want the handlers to be able to make swift and appropriate choices, obviously, and the only way to do that is to make them work through multiple scenarios with their dogs time and time again.

For one particular exercise, we'd traveled to another compound-type training area. The buildings in this compound were constructed out of cinder block and had small windows where some blocks had been knocked out of the walls. The discarded blocks lay on the ground inside the structures. For this exercise, I told the handlers to keep the dogs on leash until the moment they thought best. What I was hoping would happen was that a handler would release his dog prematurely and I could turn that into a teachable moment for everyone. I'd been standing on a few of those blocks, with my body half inside the room and half hanging out the window and onto the grassy area below. My plan was that as soon as a dog came into the room, I'd jump out the window. Then I would turn around to catch the dog that was sure to follow me out the window.

The point, of course, would be to make it clear to that handler that he'd made a poor choice. Not only had the "bad guy" (me) evaded capture, the MWD had been hurt in that fall from the window. In the exercise, the window was only 30 or so inches off the ground, so no harm would come to the dog. Of course, in real situations windows can be much higher off the ground, and dogs can't jump and bounce back the way cats can. They hit the ground and they hit hard.

Even after all these years of working with these dogs, even I sometimes underestimate just how fast they can go and get their target. On the first go-round, I had barely scrambled out of the window fully intact before the dog was literally nipping at my heels. He didn't come in and follow me through the window as I had predicted. Instead, he came tearing after me, because he had caught wind of me and scurried out the side door. He got in a few choice chews on me. Still, I was glad that I was able to illustrate for the handler, without putting a dog's well-being at risk, what might have happened if he *had* followed me out the window. I chose my profession and the risks and bite marks that go along with it, not to mention the responsibility to provide dogs that have received sound training and are in good health.

Just like humans, dogs occasionally develop nagging injuries during the course of their training from overuse of muscles. Sometimes we'll leave them behind to rest up and heal, but more often they just lag behind for a day or two to recuperate. Sometimes, though, a dog will miss an entire training cycle. When he's ready, he'll join another "class" already in the pipeline.

I'm eager to make sure that the dogs are safe and in the best possible shape to help keep our soldiers, sailors, and marines safe. I love the work I do, and I know how important it is to take the time to get things done right. We work hard and have some fun as well, but I absolutely refuse to cut corners. Very early on in my days as a dog trainer, after preparing one of my first dogs to go in theater, I received an e-mail in which one of the first handlers I trained sent me a detailed story about an operation he and his dog had been on. His words confirmed what I believed. We were on the right track; the dogs we trained and provided were making a difference. I'm proud to share his words here.

The moon sat just above the ridge of the mountain as we descended into a cutback that would lead us down into a valley. The boys adjusted their gear; the hike down into the valley was crisscrossed with barren loose rock and dense thorny brush along nothing more than a goat path. There had been a lot of activity in the area lately, the ground giving away constant sign of foot traffic that had kicked loose the rock underfoot. The terrain glowed with a greenish tint as we looked through our night-vision goggles studying the lay of the land before us, everyone alert for the slightest hint of danger. Reno was out front, his muscled lean body moving with little effort, his eyes alert, ears perked at every sound, his breath as he exhaled created a small vortex of hot humid air as it interacted with the cold dry air that surrounded him. I had been Reno's partner now for a little over a year. The bond between my dog and me was something that ran deep and was hard to truly explain. Quite simply put, I loved him and trusted my very life to him.

We were moving toward a target that was positioned on the other side of a small river that ran along the bottom of the valley floor. The area, according to our intel, was alive with enemy activity. Recent reports had a bomb maker in the area that we had been hunting for months. He had been involved in several IED incidents that had claimed American lives; if we had anything to do with it, after tonight he would no longer be able to hurt another one of our brothers or sisters. The guys had packed light.

The elevation change was thousands of feet, spread out over a dozen miles, and we had to get in and out in this cycle of darkness. Covering a dozen miles under normal circumstances is relatively easy; doing it in the dark with a massive elevation change and carrying 50 pounds of gear along with the always present chance of contact can be downright exhausting. Reno moved with purpose, his incredible senses scanning the area around him, looking for the possibility of his second-favorite thing in the world, a ball. Reno had no idea that he was out front leading the way to warn us of the danger of an IED. He simply knew that if he found explosive odor a ball would magically appear out of thin air and he would get to carry it around like a trophy for a while.

My knowledge base of explosive and human odor movement had grown a hundredfold over the last year. I knew that to best use Reno's natural capabilities I had to put him into the best position possible to take advantage of the situation, keeping mission requirements and limitations in mind. I looked at the terrain and calculated wind direction, wind speed, temperature, humidity, elevation changes, terrain formations, barometric pressure, and vegetation types and densities. Most of my concentration was on the dog. Subtle changes in his body language could give me large clues as to what was going on around us. It was up to John, walking just behind me, to scan the terrain and guide us in the right direction. We rounded a corner and the wind was suddenly blowing directly in our faces as we moved down the ridge, a stiff cold breeze that chilled me to the bone. Reno's head lifted slightly as he sniffed the new flow of air. I pictured thousands of molecules being processed by his olfactory system, and a sense of calm overcame me. He was not worried, so neither was I.

The next few hours wore on; the downhill portion of this track was starting to rub the front of my toes raw. A lot of weight at a steep angle over time will do that to even the most seasoned feet. The trail doubled back on itself as we nearly reached the valley floor. The wind was at our backs as we moved forward, sending a chill running down my spine, yet not from the cold. Everything I had learned over the last year screamed at me, this situation was developing into an almost worst-case scenario for Reno. The wind was cold and running fast from behind us down a narrow ravine that would open into the valley, pushing any odor away from us until we were on top of it. Not good.

I signaled the guys to move back a bit as Reno and I pushed forward. I would be lying if I said that my heart rate was not elevated. I was about to move through a choke point in the terrain in hostile enemy territory that was densely covered with a thick thorn-bearing bush that made the path neither quiet nor easy to see through. I gave the command for Reno to move forward and search for any hint of human or explosive odor. My weapon was raised and pointed in the general direction from which I expected a threat as I watched my boy search the area. His nose was down, sucking in all available odor, his tail up and wagging as he crisscrossed the path and moved deeper into the choke point.

I moved forward slowly, step by step, as I watched him work. Eventually we were through the high-threat area, Reno never signaled a threat. I took a deep breath and smiled.

We pushed forward again. I started to relax as we moved along the valley floor, my eyes trained on Reno, knowing that John was acting as my eyes and the rest of the boys were on their game also. We were getting close to the target when all of a sudden I stopped dead in my tracks. Reno's head had snapped around, and his tail was starting to waggle a hundred miles an hour as he worked his way back toward me. He was working the wind and had obviously detected an explosive odor. With the wind at our backs I had no idea how far back the explosive was. My breathing stopped as I scanned the ground around me with one eye and watched Reno with the other, adrenaline rushing through my system like white-hot lava. He sat 2 feet to my right and 5 feet in front of me, eyes focused on the ground, tail wagging furiously.

I quickly calculated what had happened; the wind had pushed the odor in a narrow scent cone out in front of us. By the time explosive molecules were available for Reno to pick up, he had already walked past the buried IED. My mind ran through a thousand possibilities before I settled on the most likely scenario being a pressure plate in our path with the explosives buried just off the track but still plenty close enough to kill anyone standing on that plate. I carefully circled around the area and then called Reno to me, making sure he would not cross the area where I was guessing the explosives had been laid. I tossed him a ball and gave him a quick pat as my heart and breathing rate returned to near normal. We took a quick GPS reading, marked the location, and moved on.

It took us another hour to reach our target location, which proved to be yet another wrong lead, or at the very least untimely information. The villagers were on edge. They had sent a call out to all local fighters, so it was time for us to leave, and fast. Our extraction point was at the leeward edge of the next ridge, but we were running short on time and moved with purpose. Ten minutes into our climb out we received information that a large group of Taliban fighters were descending on the valley. An hour later, the backs of my legs were burning, my heart racing, the cold nothing more than an afterthought as my body superheated the clothes covering it. Reno was starting to slow down; he is a specimen of a dog, in incredible shape, his muscles shredded from countless hours of training in environments that simulate our theater of operation.

I had to call a halt, resting a few minutes while Reno caught his breath. We set up a perimeter quickly. Each man was on edge, yet they all looked calm and relaxed; there was a smile on a couple of faces as sweat clung to their clothes. It is at times like this that I reflect upon the company I am keeping on this mountainside in some third world country, being hunted by a number of enemy that far outnumber us. I would choose to be nowhere else in the world; each one here was my brother.

Reno drank some water from my canteen, his tongue dripping water all over me as he licked my face quickly. I smiled and pushed him away gently, then patted his side quietly. I gave him a few minutes, then put him back to work. We moved back up the mountain, pushing ourselves to reach safety. A few minutes thereafter I thanked my stars above that I had given him that break. I had my eyes off of Reno as I tried to catch myself as my foot slipped on the loose, rocky terrain. When I looked up he was locked up, his body rigid as his ears pushed forward, a slight quiver in his rear left leg.

He was indicating he had detected human odor, the greatest reward my dog had.

I instantly lifted my M-4 as my eyes scanned the terrain above us; I knew without looking that John and the other guys were moving as soon as my weapon came up. Reno took off at a dead sprint and disappeared twenty feet to our left. Seconds afterward, screams came from the area. I moved forward, scanning the environment as I moved, wanting to come to Reno's aid as soon as possible but unwilling to leave behind my tactical sense. I heard three shots ring out as a Taliban fighter tried to exit the shallow cut that he and one other insurgent had been hiding in. His companion was locked in a fight with Reno; the dog was destroying him. Blood was quickly covering the man's clothes. I called Reno out of the fight and squeezed off several rounds as the man reached for his weapon. We quickly searched the area before moving on; our pace was even quicker than before, as the gunfire for sure gave away our position. Legs and lungs burned, the elevation taking its toll as we finally reached our destination.

Sitting on the edge of that mountain waiting for our ride, I looked back at the last few hours. I patted Reno's head. Twice tonight he had saved my life. Twice I owed him yet another debt of gratitude. His body shivered slightly as the cold wind bit into him. Now that we weren't moving, the cold settled quickly. I pulled off my coat and wrapped him in it, pulling his body against mine to keep him warm. Tonight he had saved my life. Tonight he had saved my brothers' lives.

10

DISTINCT PERSONALITIES

Luke glanced behind him. All he could see was water. He and his handler, my friend Wayne, were more than 500 yards from shore. I was there, too, along with some other handlers and their dogs. When Luke turned his face back toward us, I could see the fear and panic in his eyes. Dogs are smart and have great instincts for self-preservation. I could tell he was pretty much done swimming and was panicking about how much longer this training exercise was going to take and how much farther away from land they were going to get. He was anxious about when he would be able to stop, get out of the cold water, and be back on shore.

Pretty soon, Luke's panicked look turned into a sodden expression of anger. He took off after Wayne, and it was clear he was bent on destroying something—or someone. It was as if that dog had decided that if he was going down, he was taking someone with him.

Because I've seen this with dozens of other dogs in this kind of situation, I also knew that, in Luke's mind, he was viewing anything bobbing alongside him in the water as something he could climb up on and be safe. So Luke was mad at Wayne, but he also saw him as a piece of land to rest on.

For the next fifteen minutes or so, I thought I was in the middle of Jaws 1D—1 Dog. Wayne did his best to fend off that dog, flanking him while Luke turned tight circles, his front paws working like a razor-

sharp paddlewheel, his bared teeth white and pointy like shark teeth. Every time Luke got close to Wayne, Wayne pushed Luke's hindquarters away from him. When he couldn't get to his flanks, Wayne had to resort to pushing at Luke's neck and the side of his head. It was a battle of wills the rest of us kept our eyes on while we also kept going.

— —

I'd been in that position myself, with dogs who were so scared that the rate of their paddling, combined with their desire to climb on top of you to get up out of the water, could potentially turn you into human coleslaw and had you at wit's end. Luke was all that and pretty bite aggressive, too. The thing that Wayne couldn't do, and none of the trainee handlers could do, in this situation or in any other, was to give in and let the dog have his way. If you did, you had a major problem on your hands. That dog would then, in his mind, go up thirty places on the mental totem pole that signified his status. Cave in to a dog like one of these just once, and your life could be torturous. As it was, many of us ended up getting parts of our bodies raked by the thumbs and dewclaws of a panicked swimming dog, and those raised welts were just another way that we all earned our stripes.

It's a given that human SEAL team members need to be comfortable and way beyond competent in the water due to the nature of the work they do. The same is true of SEAL team canines. Most of the dogs that we purchase have had some "exposure" to the water. We quickly find out that that term can mean anything from drinking water to actively swimming in it. Like most of the training a dog has received before we acquire him, those experiences haven't necessarily been the most positive, reward-based ones. As a result, we have to do a lot of reward-based work with a dog we acquire to get him to be comfortable with swimming. As with most things we teach, we start out small and basic and advance from there. We toss a ball in the water and let the dog chase it. We toss it farther and farther over time so those first few opportunities in the water are the equivalent of wading. We do this before we get into the high-pawing, paddling, splashing technique that we see some of them employ early on.

Eventually, after many repetitions and rewards, we get to the point where the dogs are ready to go out with their handlers on the kind of swim that Luke and Wayne were participating in. It's what I call a "conditioning swim." We go out as a group, the handlers and dogs in a loose pack, with the dogs on a modified type of lead. While the dogs may be more at ease in the water at this point, they have also definitely developed a "near to the beach" comfort level. So we stretch them out in the ocean or in Balboa Bay or elsewhere to the point where they can no longer see the shoreline.

That day with Luke and Wayne, we were all headed on an out-and-back swim beyond a buoy. As painful as it was for Wayne to endure Luke's panic, and as rough as that swim was for Luke, it was far better that they go through this on the so-called practice field than in the real game. The price we'd pay in lives lost if a dog panicked during a swimming insertion was not something I wanted to think about but was certainly something I wanted to prevent. As tiresome and frustrating as it might have been to do swim training with the dogs in an environment that is relatively foreign to them, it made me realize just how important patience and follow-through were in doing this kind of training.

As I've said, dogs are smart, and Luke was especially smart. He was also notorious for being the most acrobatic dog of his training group. If dogs could be gymnasts, Luke would have been the equivalent of both the Hamm brothers. The things this dog could do with his body, how he could flex, twist, and contort himself to make sure that his mouth was pointed in the right direction, were the stuff of legend.

As I also said, Luke was pretty bite aggressive. All these qualities allowed him to excel at apprehension training. In fact, one of the challenges a decoy had during an apprehension training exercise with Luke was catching him. He was always really, really good at feinting and faking. He'd come at you, looking for sure like he was going to come at you hard, low, and left. Then, at the last split second, he'd switch it up and catch you off guard. As a decoy, you take pride in not being knocked down because you do it so often that you get good at it. You get comfortable, and then you start to get a little cocky, thinking that no dog's going to take you down. Then Luke comes along, of course.

One night a few years ago, Wayne and I were on an apprehension-training exercise with a group of about six dogs and handlers. Wayne grew up mostly in Florida and spent a lot of his early years in the swamps, tracking and hunting wild hogs using dogs. I don't know of anyone else who can read a dog like Wayne can, and I also don't know anyone else who can work as a decoy any better. He's also a trainer, and one of the German shepherds he had was titled in seven or eight different disciplines, which is an almost unheard-of accomplishment. Wayne seems to have an extrasharp sense of anticipation about what a dog is thinking of doing. So he and Luke were quite the match.

That night, just like we always did, Wayne and I headed up the mountains in advance of the others. We were "on comms," in communication with the handlers and our assistants. We got several miles out ahead of the other men and the dogs and radioed back when we selected a good hideout. Then it was time for the dogs to detect human odor and alert their handlers. Each handler would give the *"Reviere"* command, and the handler and dog would come looking for us. We were suited up, of course, wearing middle-weight bite suits with a neoprene underlayer. It's kind of like a wet suit, but the bottom layer offers additional padding. The outer layer is slick, which makes it harder for a dog to grab hold of it.

It generally takes the dogs twenty to thirty minutes to cover the few miles between our find position and their release point. We did a debrief after each dog went through his exercise, taking notes so that we could do a full-blown evaluation of each dog and handler at the completion of the entire exercise. After the first five dogs, we took a break. Then Wayne was due up as the decoy again. I looked at him and said, "You know who's coming, don't you?"

He nodded. "Yes, I do," he said, sounding both a bit prideful and on edge. It was going to be Luke.

I said, "I bet you can't *esquive* Luke." *Esquive* is a French word that means "to dodge or to sidestep."

Wayne shook his head. "I'll *esquive* him all day long."

So I said, "Okay, well, let's bet dinner on it. Winner's choice."

After a few minutes, I climbed to a little ridge where I could see better. It was a fairly well-lit night, not quite full-moon bright but close. Over the comms, about fifteen minutes before, I'd heard, "Dog out," so it was going to be just a few minutes until the action started. I sat there thinking, *All right, I can't wait to see this.*

Keep in mind, Wayne is the best decoy I've ever seen. He's so quick on his feet that, if anybody could *esquive* Luke, it would be Wayne. Honestly, I thought he had a pretty good chance of doing it. Then, when I saw Luke coming, I was a little disappointed. He was charging at Wayne from much the same direction as an earlier dog, Duke, had come at me. I knew Wayne had seen how that went down—it turned into one of those times when I thought my arm was going to be crushed. So Wayne was going to have the advantage of seeing my mistake.

Suddenly, though, still running at close to full tilt, Luke didn't come uphill at Wayne. Instead, he went around a few scrub bushes from the windward side and buttoned up back around. As a result, Wayne had to spin around fast. As any good soldier knows, it's important to take the high ground, and that's exactly what Luke did. He took Wayne completely off guard, hit him right in the chest, and just pancaked my good friend. Wayne is 6'2" and weighs between 220 and 225 pounds; Luke blitzed him as if he were a bag full of leaves.

Wayne managed to get up and finish out the exercise, but afterward he was reluctant to own up to his loss. "I knocked that one on purpose. I didn't want the dog to get hurt," he insisted.

Whatever.

"Dude," I said to Wayne, "don't give me that excuse. I want my dinner."

Wayne made good on his promise, and I also had good ammunition to throw at him for the next few weeks about how Luke outsmarted him. The combination of Luke's cunning and strength was extremely impressive.

— —

In any school there are star students, the ones whose performance in the classroom or on the playing fields makes it clear that they are going to succeed at whatever they choose to do. Sometimes they live up to those expectations, and sometimes they don't. The same is true with the dogs that we train. Every time a governmental agency, a military group, or even a private individual looking for a protection dog comes to view the prospects that I have, I mentally compile a list of the dogs that I think are the sure things among the bunch, the ones who are, undoubtedly, in my mind the ones worthy of the purchase price.

As often as not, my mental rankings are a lot like those preseason polls and predictions in football—some of them prove to be true, and nearly as many prove to be off target. Everybody who views dogs during their workouts and showings sees something slightly different. I'm biased, of course. I think that what I see in the dogs is the "truth" about them, but as the saying goes, "The customer is always right."

Because I've been involved in the breeding, training, and sale of dogs for more than fifteen years now, you might think it's easy for me to say good-bye to the dogs I've worked with. In one sense that's true. I'm glad to see them go and do what they were bred, born, and trained to do, but there's always going to be some emotional attachment to the dogs. As much as I've talked about them and their abilities, these dogs aren't machines. They all clearly have distinct personalities, like Luke.

One dog in particular, who shall remain nameless, got my attention very early in the process. Immediately after we brought him over to the United States, I went to his crate to let him out. It was like I'd released a Tasmanian devil. That dog got up on his hind legs, spun around in circles like a tornado, snapped his jaws like the maniac he was, and generally said to me, "Hello, my name is Havoc." Essentially, this dog was announcing to me that I was going to have my hands full just to get him through the most basic obedience training. As much as I've talked about what near-perfect physical specimens these dogs are, because they've been bred to preserve the high energy and tenaciousness necessary to go at it in hostile environments, they are seldom docile. I developed a tremendous amount of respect for the spastic Tas-like dog, but I can't say that I ever really developed a bond of affection for him.

That wasn't the case with one of the first dogs to work with a SEAL team. Rocket is like one of those kids you can't help admiring or hating. You know, the kid that is good-looking, athletic, and friendly. All the kids like him, the teachers and administrators get along well with him, and he never puts on airs.

On Rocket's second deployment to northern Afghanistan, near the border with Pakistan, he and his handler, Brent, arrived at a firebase that was still under construction. This was in the dead of winter in January 2007. The troops were living in open base tents while the buildings were being completed. To put it mildly, life there was a mixture of dealing with bone-chilling cold and frozen tedium.

Handlers have to be very careful about how they integrate themselves into the SEAL teams and with other military personnel. They have to be sensitive to the fact that each of their comrades brings a different set of associations and experiences to being in close contact with a MWD. Some of the men are fearful. Others are curious. Still others are disdainful out of ignorance about the roles the dogs will eventually play, and so on. For a handler and a dog, it's just like being a newbie in any situation; you have to earn the respect of your teammates.

Brent wanted to make sure that everybody understood from the get-go that Rocket was there to be a help and not an impediment. He also let them know that his relationship with Rocket was a kind of one-off—that the two of them had forged a real bond in the nearly two years they'd worked together before being deployed.

In order to respect the other troops and their safety and their personal space and gear, Brent and Rocket needed segregated housing. Basically, they needed their own room. The Seabees, the navy's construction battalion who were building the firebase, were assigned to build a partition with a door within the shared tent where Brent and Rocket were to rack out.

As luck would have it, the pair was already assigned to a tent where the Seabees were quartered. In the first couple of days, before the wall could be built, Rocket did what dogs do: He foraged for food. The Seabees had a few snacks that Rocket sniffed out and consumed. Brent apologized, and he could tell that a few of the guys were cool with it, while others looked a little anxious. One thing was clear, no one was going to complain too loudly or confront the fierce-looking dog. A compromise was reached. Until the wall and door could go up to keep Rocket away from their stuff, they'd just put it out of his reach.

Brent noticed that as the days went on, and some of the guys in the tent had to get out of bed in the middle of the night to do a watch, they'd come back and find Rocket sacked out in their rack, snoring away. The displaced guys let the dog keep on sleeping there. Brent found a couple of guys sleeping on the floor while Rocket happily snoozed more comfortably. At first Brent thought that they didn't dare wake up and roust Rocket out of their rack because they were afraid of him. He finally asked some of the guys about it. They said that they didn't mind Rocket sleeping in their beds; they actually kind of liked the idea of having him around. Rocket became a kind of mascot, a four-legged, furry roommate, and he took full advantage of the attention and affection he got. Not every MWD has his temperament; there was just something about his big ears and quizzical expression that let you know that he was easygoing when off duty. The only complaint the guys had was that Rocket sometimes farted while sitting in the middle of everybody, an "end result" of them sneaking him foods he wasn't accustomed to getting. Not that much different from the rest of the guys, in reality.

The wall that was supposed to keep Rocket from the rest of the guys never really got built. At first the framing went up, then it was sheeted, but no door was hung. The Seabees and others confessed that they liked having Rocket around, and they knew that once that door went up, he'd be separated from them. In time, the wall came down completely. The guys were told by the officer in charge (OIC) that it had to go back up and a door had to be installed. Once again, the guys came up with excuses to delay building it. Finally the wall went up, but for the duration of that deployment, no door was ever hung, and Rocket was free to mingle with the rest of them. Maybe he was like having a bit of home for some of the guys, but I do know that as much as that, it was a tribute to Rocket's amiability. His big brown eyes melted a lot of hearts and earned him his share of treats. By the end of their deployment, Brent told me, he had a list of names a mile long of guys who wanted first dibs on one of Rocket's puppies.

—◆—

Some say that dogs are nature's greatest con artists, that they've finagled for themselves a pretty soft gig compared to most animals. They're certainly not parasites, though, and the kinds of relationship we and canines have negotiated over the years have truly proved beneficial, just as Rocket's role both in the field and on station did. All I will say is that whatever ease dogs have accrued as a result of their domestication, we've frequently asked a lot from them in return. That's particularly true as it applies to our long history of using them in warfare. Another way to look at it is this. The people we allow to take advantage of our kindness are generally not strangers— they're usually family members and close friends. We benefit from those relationships, or have benefited from them in the past and hope to in the future. So really, nobody is truly being conned. You can also look at it from the dog's perspective. We've taken advantage of their good nature and their desire to share their companionship with us, and we've used them to our advantage. Everything's a trade-off, I suppose, but in my estimation, we humans have come out far ahead in the canine-human transaction.

11

THE BOND AT BOTH ENDS
OF THE LEASH

A dog can have a great personality and be very well bred, athletic, and smart. That still leaves us with a lot of work to do before a dog is ready to be deployed. A key component of that work includes the dog's handler. Not unlike the dog that will be at the other end of the leash, each handler has to go through his own extensive training. I've spent a lot of time training both handlers and dogs, sometimes separately and sometimes together. I've found that even though someone is a great SEAL team member, that doesn't mean he'll function well as a handler, and just because a dog has earned his title, that doesn't mean he'll make a great SOF dog.

A handler and a dog that do qualify as individuals still have to function seamlessly as a team within the larger SEAL team and the battlefield into which they are deployed. There needs to be extraordinary trust, understanding, and respect between a handler and his dog, like the kind Brent and Rocket have for each other. Another amazing duo is Aaron and Castor. These two serve as a template for the kind of heart and mind necessary to take on the task of being a Navy SEAL handler-and-dog team. Aaron's dedication to his dog differs only slightly from the devotion that most pet owners feel toward the four-legged friend in their lives.

Like me, Aaron grew up knowing what he wanted to do with his life. Living in South Dakota, just outside Rapid City, he couldn't see Mount Rushmore, but he had a much closer and living, breathing example of our country's greatness—his grandfather. Aaron's grandfather was a member of the "Greatest Generation," meaning he grew up during the Great Depression and went on to fight on the battlefields of World War II. Like my own grandfather, and like so many others, he didn't sit around spinning yarns about his exploits. In fact, no one else in Aaron's family except for Aaron seemed to place much emphasis on Grandpa Jim's experiences. "I was just extremely interested," Aaron said. "There was something about the military that I liked, so I started asking him about World War II. And once he started talking, he opened up and just told me all kinds of amazing stories."

Aaron's grandfather was one of those patriotic Americans who enlisted the day after Pearl Harbor and became a boatswain's mate on three different ships. He was also one of those fortunate Americans who served for the duration, including a lengthy stint aboard the USS *Portland*, which saw duty in major naval battles in the Pacific. From Guadalcanal to Corregidor to Okinawa, the men aboard the USS *Portland* served with distinction. Aaron's grandfather didn't glorify the war, and Aaron recalled some of the horrific elements of naval combat he was told about, but mostly he remembered what his grandfather told him about the camaraderie among the crewmen and the lifelong friendships he made. "Basically, he said that those experiences were the best and worst times of his life," Aaron said.

Aaron described himself as a rambunctious, semidelinquent kid who frequently found himself in trouble. That led to his desire to join the military. "I wanted to be sneaky," he said, "and I thought Special Operations were cool." He'd heard about the marines' Force Reconnaissance from a neighbor who was a part of that group and was initially interested in finding out more about them, but that changed when a friend's brother returned from the U.S. Naval Academy over the Christmas holidays. Aaron had never heard of the SEALs, but he began to do research. "I was big into swimming," he recalled. "I loved doing martial arts, so as soon as I read about the Navy SEALs, that was it." From the time he was thirteen years old, Aaron knew that he one day wanted to belong to an elite SEAL team. He told himself that as soon as he graduated from high school, he was going to join the navy.

As much as he liked swimming, Aaron wasn't on the swim team, but he did play water polo. Actually, "play" isn't exactly the right word. "Because I didn't have the cardio fitness of the other guys and couldn't even complete all the practice laps, the coaches just told me to go into the other pool while the other guys practiced and scrimmaged," he said. "I kind of realized I was a terrible swimmer." Eventually Aaron overcame that, but it took some time and a lot of hard work.

"I'm a big reader," Aaron said, "and I love to research things before I get into them, so I knew what I was getting into when I decided I wanted to become a SEAL team member. But I really underestimated how hard it was going to be. When I showed up for BUD/S training, I wasn't ready. When I showed up at BUD/S, out of a class of 186 or so guys, I was the second slowest runner in the class. After the first day, the slowest guy quit, so I became *the* slowest."

Aaron can laugh about the situation now, but at the time, it took all his mental strength to get through it. He'd enlisted at the tail end of 1993, then spent nearly three years training to become and then serve as a corpsman in a military medical unit before he graduated from BUD/S in 1997. As a member of his SEAL team, he served initially in the U.S. Pacific Command Theater out of Guam. "We traveled a lot doing Foreign Internal Defense training with other countries' special ops guys," he recalled. "I was in Thailand, Malaysia, Singapore, Australia, the Philippines."

In 2004, on his third deployment to Iraq, he was doing Direct Action Missions, hunting down high-value targets there. Later, like me, he transitioned from chasing bad guys to protecting good guys, serving on a personal security detail for members of the interim government. After his fourth platoon deployment, he was assigned shore duty for one year. That didn't sit well with him. "I had a desk job working with the medical department," he said. "I basically was responsible for assigning other corpsmen to be on hand when the SEALs were doing training exercises. If a SEAL platoon went to the range to shoot, they needed a medic there. I was the guy who sent a non-SEAL corpsman to those locations."

Aaron wasn't happy being a desk jockey, but orders were orders. One day in 2006, he was asked to send a corpsman to accompany a SEAL team doing dog training. Aaron sent one, but his curiosity was piqued. "Even before our guy came back and told me about how awesome it was to see what they were doing with these dogs, I was asking questions when the request came in," Aaron said. "After he told me about it, I knew I had to see this for myself."

The next time a corpsman was needed, Aaron tagged along for a day to watch the training. He watched the handlers working the dogs on explosive-detection scenarios and came away impressed with the dogs' capabilities. Later, watching bite-work exercises, he was even more impressed. He'd heard about MWDs and had seen a few in Iraq during his four deployments there, but seeing them up close made a major impression on him.

"I'd worked briefly in Iraq with dogs from conventional forces—marines and army—but basically we told their handlers how things were going to go," Aaron recalled. "We were going to go hit some house, and if a bad guy ran out the back, you sent the dog after him. That was the limit of my interaction with dogs to that point. After seeing those SEAL training exercises, I realized there was a lot more they could do."

He found out from the OIC that they were looking for volunteers. Aaron asked the question that every military man considering volunteering for a program would, "What's the catch?"

He was told there was none. He would have to make a two-year commitment at minimum. He'd be given a dog, be trained as a handler himself, then get to deploy. "That was the magic word," he said. "This was still wartime, and the dogs were guaranteed to deploy to the hottest spots because, obviously, that's where they were needed the most."

Aaron wanted to make certain he had things clear in his mind. "So I said to the OIC, 'So you're telling me if I come over here right now, you're going to give me a dog and I'm going to get to go to combat?' When the OIC said yes, I said, 'Oh yeah, I am there.'"

In 2007, Aaron was one of the first handlers outside of Seal Team Six to be working with dogs on the East Coast. The program was so new at the time that, as Aaron put it, "you could have asked any SEAL if there was a dog team, and most would have said no. A few would have said, 'We don't have one, but Team Six does.' Basically, we existed before anyone outside our group knew we existed."

Fortunately for Aaron, and for the dog team members, he was a corpsman by training, and that likely contributed to his transfer request being approved. He served double duty as a corpsman and handler. His medical duties also included caring for the dogs, and he served as a kind of veterinary technician for them. Eventually he took as many courses in canine medicine as he could to get up to speed.

Not everything Aaron had been told by the OIC proved to be true, but that was okay. The program was in its infancy but was well funded. Along with other members of the team, Aaron got to travel to Germany and Holland to observe the basic training regimens the dogs underwent. Aaron needed that kind of exposure since he had never worked with dogs. His family kept dogs as pets, but he wasn't what he'd consider "a dog guy." After the first few months of training, he was hooked. "I fell in love with it," he said. "This was the best time in my career."

Part of that had to do with being liberated from a desk job, but a lot of it had to do with his interactions with his dog, Castor. Aaron laughingly talks about Castor being a first-round draft pick. At the time, the Special Operations Command realized that there was a great need for dogs all across the SOF spectrum. Vendors were found who could supply dogs, and then representatives of the Green

Berets, MARSOF (Marine Special Operations Forces), the SEAL teams, and the Rangers all went on-site to view and select the dogs. At each "draft" camp, one group would be given the first pick, and then at a later one, another group would get to pick first, and so on. Aaron knew going in that the West Coast teams had the first pick.

Before the skills demonstration began, they got to view the candidates. "It was an extremely tight-quarters kennel," said Aaron, "and the smell was horrendous. The sound level was ridiculous as well. We were all walking through there, and some of the dogs were barking, some were spinning tight circles, and just about every one of them was going nuts in some way. Then I saw Castor. He was sitting there staring back at this group of strangers staring at him. He was just chilling, and nothing fazed him at all. I called him over so that I could pet him, but he just kept staring at me like, 'Yeah, whatever, I'm not doing that.' So I bent down and looked at him, and I knew he was the one. I liked his calm demeanor. I'm a pretty calm guy, and pairing with someone like me had a lot of appeal. I told myself I was going to keep my eye on this one."

During the selection and bite work, Castor stood out. Later, the trainer/vendors confirmed that Castor had great skills. The rest of the Special Operations guys seemed dubious.

"We were all relatively new at this and didn't have a lot of experience with training dogs and none with working in the field with them," said Aaron. "Most of the other guys wanted one of those really big and aggressive types that had been so disruptive in the kennel. What convinced me that Castor was the right one was when we got to do some early socialization work with them."

For this part of the selection process, Castor was muzzled and led out of his kennel. Aaron got Castor to lie down and then joined him on the ground. He'd hop over Castor's back and then wrap his arms around him. The point was to see what kind of aggression the dog would demonstrate toward a handler. Castor took it all in stride. Aaron also picked Castor up, something that makes even the mildest of dogs edgy, but again Castor showed no discomfort.

"A lot of these dogs, you touch them and they want to eat you. They're just angry animals," Aaron explained. "But Castor was like, 'Yep. Just another day.' I knew this dog was perfect for me because he was a superstar in the drills and he was completely social."

Though Aaron wasn't an experienced dog trainer, he innately understood how important the bond of trust between a dog and his handler is. That Castor allowed himself to be touched and picked up without complaint meant that he'd adapt easily to working with a new person and that the basic level of trust of humans was already in place. Castor sensed that this person wasn't going to hurt him. That trait was demonstrated later on during helicopter training in preparation for fast-roping insertions.

Aaron had strapped Castor into his tactical vest, which is equipped with a handle on the top of it. To expose the dog to this kind of environment takes some time. Initially, just getting a dog used to the sound of the engines and the wind-whipped air is enough. Eventually, though, you have to get the dog in the chopper and off the ground. Most dogs are resistant to not having all four paws firmly planted on the ground. So you can imagine how difficult it is to get a dog to climb out of a helicopter's bay and voluntarily go into thin air. Aaron and the other early handler trainees employed a sink-or-swim approach.

"I had to take Castor and grab the handle of his vest, lift him up, and then dangle him out over the lip of the helicopter," Aaron said. "He thought I was throwing him out of the bird, and he freaked out—paws thrashing, torso twisting. Once I let go of him, and of course he's tethered to me, so he isn't going far. He dropped a couple of inches and then just hung there. He was immediately totally calm, and I imagined he was thinking, 'Oh, okay, cool. This is fine. Dad's got me.'"

That kind of trust is a perfect example of what is essential in a relationship between an MWD and his handler. Castor and Aaron had it from the outset, and that bond only hardened and deepened as time went on. Much of that was due to Aaron's dedication. Though admittedly not a dog person when he started and more someone who saw the SEAL team's use of dogs as a way out of a desk job and back into combat, Aaron used his research and reading skills to help him learn even more about how to work with dogs. Unlike some of his fellow SEAL handlers, Aaron began using positive reinforcement early on, partly based on his research and partly because of his relationship with Castor. "He was my friend," said Aaron. "I didn't want to have to correct him. I didn't want to have to jerk him around. If I could make him more receptive and get better results without all those negative punishments, then, even though I was going against the grain, nobody could say anything against me. To me, it wasn't enough to go through the handler program and get dogs to do their jobs. I wanted to know how a dog thought, how he learned, and what I can get him to do without inflicting pain on him."

Aaron took the same approach to his job as a dog handler as he did everything else in his career as a SEAL. He knew that the job the dogs would eventually do was too important for him not to learn as much as he possibly could. At that point in the early development of the program, the people training the handlers only had fairly limited experience with old-school methods of training and disciplining dogs. Aaron was concerned that those methods might have their limits.

"I want to be the best at every single thing I do," he said. "I also have a lot of natural curiosity, so I wanted to learn as much as I could. More important, if I show up in Afghanistan or wherever with my dog, and I introduce myself to the unit I'm assigned to, I have a great deal of responsibility on my shoulders. If that dog accidentally bites one of my guys, or if that dog doesn't detect some explosives and guys get wounded or killed, that's on me. That's my fault, not the dog's. And what if that guy who got bit has to be sent home, and then his replacement comes along and something happens to him?"

The downside of having that kind of bond with a dog, if there is one at all, may be in what Aaron felt as additional pressure—not just for his fellow soldiers but with the dog who he'd come to care so much about. "When you're walking point with your dog, you're the first one to see bad guys. If anything happens to anyone else, it's your fault. That's a lot of pressure to carry around. Even so, when I'm out walking point and I've got my dog in front of me looking for explosives, I'm also worried about *his* well-being," Aaron explained. "When you're doing that detection work, your sole focus is on wind direction. If you're patrolling down a trail and there's only one way to enter this trail that is tactically sound and you're unlucky enough that on that particular night the wind is at your back and not pushing those odors toward you, the stress gets even more intense. Castor could step on a pressure plate even before he smelled those explosives just as easily as a human could—some of those antipersonnel pressure plates are that sensitive. The thought of getting that dog hurt, because he trusted me enough to go there, added to the burden. We love each other. I can honestly say that if Castor got badly injured, I would have as hard a time dealing with that as I would if something happened to other team members."

Part of the reason why Castor and Aaron bonded is the qualities of courage and tenacity that dog possessed. For instance, on one particular training exercise, Castor and Aaron had been moving through a heavily wooded area. They had been patrolling along a road during a bite-work exercise when Castor came on human odor. Aaron released him, and Castor ripped through the woods in pursuit. Aaron watched as Castor leapt through some brush and then disappeared. Eventually Aaron caught up to the trainer in the bite suit, fully engaged with the dog near a rocky outcropping. Blood spattered the gray stone. Aaron began calling for Castor to release the trainer, fearful that the dog had punctured both the bite suit and the human underneath it. Instead, what he saw was blood gushing out of his dog's chest. On closer examination, he could see that Castor had impaled himself on a sharp stick. The stick had entered the dog's body with such force that it was still underneath his skin, extending from the entry point on his chest down his flank for about twelve inches. As horrified as he was, Aaron was also impressed that a wound that severe hadn't slowed Castor down one bit.

Regulations required that the dogs be kept on-site, even in the case of an injury. In order to treat Castor, Aaron had to drive home to get additional equipment he kept there. He also brought along his wife, a surgical nurse. In the field, Aaron had removed most of the stick, but he could feel that more was still buried beneath his skin and fur. Castor didn't show great signs of distress, so Aaron didn't anesthetize him. Even without a muzzle on the dog, Aaron and his wife felt safe performing minor surgery on Castor. They removed the remaining pieces of stick, flushed the wound with various antiseptics, and then sutured him up.

Castor was out of commission for only a week. Obviously, not every handler can provide his dog with that kind of medical treatment, but it's a potent example of how essential it is that a dog trusts his handler.

In ways large and small, Aaron took care of Castor, and his reward for that was a dog whose performance in the field was outstanding. Aaron also went above and beyond some of the training standards of those early days. He trained Castor to follow a laser pointer's red dot. Dogs are capable of following our gaze. If we first engage a dog to get his attention and then look elsewhere, the dog will look where we look. In the field that has limited applications, but getting a dog to follow a laser pointer's red dot is extremely useful.

Here are the basics of how it worked. In the field, Aaron would get Castor's attention, show him the laser apparatus, point the beam at something specific, and Castor would go to that point. If, for example, Aaron issued the apprehend command to Castor but there were multiple targets in front of them, Aaron could point the laser on the person he wanted Castor to apprehend. Or Aaron could point the laser at a particular door or wall, either in full daylight or in pitch blackness, from a distance of 200 to 300 yards. If the detection command was then issued, Castor would go to the lasered area as soon as he was released from his leash.

That's a particularly effective clearing method. If Castor did not detect any explosives by that door or wall, the team members could then place ladders against those walls to climb over them, or use a breaching charge to blow a door, without worrying about any IEDs being present.

Aaron also pushed Castor's apprehension training to the point where he felt 100 percent confident that his dog would not bite anyone dressed similarly to his handler—unless instructed to do so. That was especially important because frequently when on a mission, Castor would enter a confined area with numerous people in it after having been given the command to apprehend someone. Given the potential confusion, a less disciplined dog might take on anyone. Aaron is convinced of, and has seen evidence of, Castor's ability to distinguish friend from foe. On numerous patrols in Afghanistan, in crowded bazaars, in homes, and in open areas, Castor has learned to sort through the individuals there, running through the legs of people, in pursuit of the bad guy.

--- * ---

Aaron and Castor worked together on two deployments in Afghanistan, primarily detecting explosives. The two were able to utilize the tools they had learned in training to clear buildings and provide protection for the troops with whom they served.

In some ways Aaron and Castor's story is unique. Each of their individual attributes meshed well together. They were there at the beginning of the program, before I began providing and training dogs for the teams. Castor is retired from active duty, and Aaron is a trainer at BUD/S. Castor lives with Aaron and his family. When I visited them and sat and talked with Aaron, Castor lay at his feet, waiting. Aaron told me that as soon as we were finished, he was going to go to work and Castor was going with him. That day's training activities for the next class of SEALs involved some beach running, and Castor liked that. Other days, Castor can be found at Aaron's wife's office. He's taken over a couch there, and he's content to watch her type away at her computer. Once the tapping sounds end, he looks at her and she at him. It's lunchtime or break time, and that means a walk around the area. A tennis ball is frequently involved. At quitting time, the two head home, and then Castor hangs out there with both his mom and his dad. He's seldom alone, and Aaron and his wife take him just about everywhere they go. He's adjusted well to his downtime and is about as content as any dog can be in knowing that he's well cared for and respected for what he's done for one man and one woman and for their, and his, country.

PART III

ADVENTURES IN BATTLE

— 12 —

CAIRO AND LLOYD:
AMONG THE FIRST

The Sunni Triangle, Iraq

Cairo and his handler, Lloyd, saw a human figure dash across the dark, desolate landscape, beating feet toward a hut. The other team member with them raised his weapon, but Lloyd stopped him. He said, "I'm going to let Cairo go."

They were in an area near Lake Tharthar, a large lake that sits in the center of an irregularly shaped rectangle formed by the cities of Haditha, Tikrit, Samarra, and Ramadi. Despite the area's proximity to water, it was nonetheless typical of a lot of the Iraqi landscape. There was a seemingly endless monotony of sand, broken up by a few rolling hills, palm trees, and scrub. The plant life stuck out like bits of stems in a huge pile of brown rice. There were also low-walled buildings and flat roofs that gave Lloyd the impression they were moving through a boot print, a place where everything had somehow been squashed down and compressed. The area had been hit with a severe drought, and the fields lay fallow.

"It was like being in a ghost town in an old Western movie, except there weren't any doors slapping in the breeze with their hinges squealing," Lloyd recalled when I paid him and Cairo a visit. "It was eerie quiet. At this point our platoon had gotten thin, and we were moving in ones and twos. I was with Cairo and one other team member. The wind was

crossing, and the dog seemed to pick up something. He was air-scenting, his nose up, and just kind of trembling like they do.

"You had to figure that anybody running around out here had to be up to something," said Lloyd. Even though the dictator Saddam Hussein had been deposed, the area was home to some of his strongest supporters. This was one of the hottest zones in the war, and the intermingling of religious conservatives, various insurgent groups, al Qaeda members, and fierce anti-American sentiment made life that much more difficult (to put it mildly) for U.S. troops there. The efforts to clear dozens and dozens of small towns spread throughout the region were critical to the overall effort to curb insurgency violence and to provide support for the interim government in Iraq.

So Lloyd unleashed Cairo, and the dog went tearing after that lone figure, running away from Lloyd's position. Even with his night-vision goggles on, it wasn't so easy for Lloyd to follow the dog as he ran. "I could see the clouds of sand he was kicking up but not a whole lot else at that point," Lloyd recalled. "He was flooding down, and I could just make out the 'target' going into one of the buildings, nothing more than a hut, really."

At that point, Lloyd and his teammate followed Cairo to the entrance. Cairo hadn't indicated any odor; if he had, he would have sat down. Instead, he had just stood at the door with his tail fanning. Deciding, then, that it was safe to approach the hut, and using techniques they'd been taught, practiced, and employed hundreds of times, Lloyd and his teammate followed Cairo inside.

Cairo sat down immediately. They were face-to-face with a dozen or so Iraqi women, children, and men. Upon seeing the soldiers and the dog, the Iraqis immediately all put their hands in the air.

"Cairo could have gone blasting in there and gone after any one of them," Dave said, explaining the importance of how the dog had behaved. "It could have just been a really bad situation for us. In that area especially, we were trying to win hearts and minds. In the Sunni Triangle you could just feel that vibe, that distrust and most likely hatred being directed at us from all over. I couldn't imagine what would have happened if Cairo had done what he'd been trained to do when he finds people, namely his apprehension bite work. But he had some sense, that dog. He *just sat there, looking fierce as hell, and nobody moved. I could tell they were all scared. They sat there wide-eyed and looking like they were seeing the devil, but Cairo just held them there."*

Lloyd and his teammate did a quick search of the room and a check on the Iraqis.

"Things could have gone down worse in so many ways, but with Cairo leading us in there, we knew that we didn't have to worry about our access point being rigged or even someone fleeing from that location," Lloyd went on. *"We took the guy we'd seen running into that building in for questioning. We never found out the result of that, but we knew this. The guy was alive, and he might have also provided valuable intel to us, all because of Cairo. Without Cairo being there, we would have likely opened fire. Who knows how many other people might have been wounded? I can't say that Cairo saved our lives in this case, but he helped save some of our credibility. And we were able to fully demonstrate our operational commitment in the area. He helped us let folks know that we weren't going to come in there to hurt people and destroy their lives. The great thing about dogs is that they are a nonlethal force. Our being able to safely apprehend that man who was running was important."*

——◆——

During that same operation, over a three-day stretch, Lloyd and his platoon continued their search of buildings in the same area. Cairo went into more than fifty compounds and countless structures to search for explosives. That kind of repetition can dull your awareness and your sense of potential dangers lurking. Lloyd was well aware that, especially under these conditions, complacency could set in despite anyone's best efforts to fight against it.

"If you've never cleared a building, you can't know how taxing that is mentally and to some extent physically," Lloyd said. "That was especially true on that deployment, because we'd heard reports of all kinds of insurgent activity in the area, and from car bombs to snipers to IEDs to ambushes, we'd suffered some pretty heavy casualties. That weighs on your mind anytime you go into some building. Having Cairo on point eased a lot of that anxiety over the unknown.

He'd proved himself to the platoon while doing those road sweeps. They knew that they could trust that Cairo would hit on either the bad guys or their weapons or explosives. Going into a room wondering is not the best way to do it. Cairo minimized that worry."

Cairo remained at the top of his game, too, never giving in to complacency. Each time he approached a new structure he acted as alert as if it were the first and only one he had searched. This proved to be extremely valuable, as Lloyd explained. "We entered yet another of the small stone structures," he said, "and at first glance, it looked just like the previous thirty-five of them had. There was a wood floor, a carpet, a few pieces of furniture, and not a whole lot more. Cairo did his thing, and he hit on odor and just sat right down in the middle of one room. We checked it before moving it, but once a table was moved to one side, and Cairo stayed right on that spot, we figured something had to be under the floor."

They removed some of the flooring, and in the space between the floor joists they found a cache of weapons and ammunition.

"You know, in conventional warfare, if you find a few AKs and dozens of rounds, that's probably not a big deal," Lloyd said. "But fighting the way we were, in small teams, and not knowing if any of the Iraqi nationals were insurgents or with al Qaeda, getting those few guns and rounds was huge. All it takes is one weapon and one round, and somebody could be killed."

— • —

In the time before Cairo came up with these finds he and Lloyd had already worked on miles and miles of road clearance, looking for IEDs. Lloyd remembered it this way. "We did so many that it started to blur together. Cairo was just working and working. After a while, I noticed that he would start to show signs of anxiety whenever I wanted him to load up in a vehicle, let alone a helo."

That was a strong indication that the dog was getting stressed. As Lloyd put it, "He definitely loved his helo rides. A lot of the other dogs got spooked in training, but not Cairo. He'd see one sitting there, rotors going or not, and he'd take off like a shot. He always wanted to be the first one on. Or if he saw them coming in to land, he'd spin circles in excitement. I'd just let him loose once they touched ground, and he would jump in the hold and sit in your seat, happy as could be."

In country, Lloyd and Cairo hadn't experienced any helo-related close calls or anything similar, so Lloyd reasoned that Cairo couldn't be associating bad things with the transport machines themselves. There was nothing Lloyd could point to precisely to explain the cause of Cairo's reluctance to mount up. He knew that Cairo was fine physically, and, importantly he'd noted no decline in the dog's capabilities to detect explosives. Cairo's mood wasn't any different either.

Lloyd suspected that Cairo's negative associations with vehicles and choppers might have had something to do with the change in the nature of their operation. Those miles and miles of road clearing were accompanied by search after search through compounds, most of which were empty but nevertheless required careful detection work. For a short while, Cairo had made no finds.

"I wondered if maybe he was like a lot of dogs," Lloyd said. "When you throw something for them to fetch and they can't find it, they get upset. They've failed to retrieve, and that's just not their nature."

He realized that Cairo's long few days of no hits did roughly coincide with his newfound reluctance to mount up. Regardless of the cause, the effect of a delay to board was potentially dangerous enough that Lloyd knew he had to break that chain of Cairo's associating vehicles with not finding anything. He decided he needed to do some in-field retraining work with the dog.

Lloyd had worked with Cairo long enough that he sensed this wasn't a case where a correction, a negative consequence, was going to achieve the desired goal of getting Cairo more comfortable with climbing into an armored personnel carrier, a helo, or anything else that moved. Lloyd figured that he had to take a few steps back from the actual boarding routine and replace Cairo's new negative associations with positive ones.

"Cairo was, and is, a ball dog," Lloyd explained. "Like most of the dogs in the program, his prey drive was off the charts. That meant ball chasing was a huge reward for him."

Lloyd put Cairo's vest on him and let him play with a ball for a bit. Then he attached his lead and repeated the ball-playing scenario. With every activity that led up to going operational and then actually getting into a vehicle, he let Cairo get his reward. The point was that if Cairo had those positive associations with every step up to and including getting into a vehicle, he'd get over his stalled entrances. Lloyd's retraining worked, and within a few days, Cairo was back on track. Shortly after that, his string of no finds came to an end, too.

Lloyd and Cairo had not always understood and trusted each other that way. In fact, shortly after they were first paired in training in 2008, this duo got off to a rather rocky start.

As part of a drill to simulate an actual firefight to accustom Cairo to the potential reality of what he would face when deployed, Lloyd had been firing his Heckler and Koch MK 23 Mod 0. The next thing he knew, in an instant, the leashed dog was on him, his jaws snapping, spit flying, and the sound of his fierce barking a counterpoint to the sound of the other trainees' weapons discharging.

"I didn't know what was going on," Lloyd recalled. "I knew that Cairo was a bit gun-shy, but to have him turn on me like that was a bit of a surprise. I was out there without a bite suit on, and this dog was giving me his best. I had to throw a few punches at him to try to subdue him. Here I was in the desert in eastern California locked in hand-to-hand, well, hand-to-jaw combat with this 75-pound dog I'd only been working with for a few weeks. Finally I was able to wrestle him to the ground, and I had my hands around his neck. His muscles are so well developed, it was like I had a giant anaconda snake in my grip. I kept choking and choking, and finally he submitted. I'd been around dogs long enough to know that I had to let up immediately. It was like he'd said 'uncle,' tapped out like a wrestler might or whatever. If I kept going, his brain would switch from 'okay, you got me' mode to 'okay, this is a life-and-death struggle and I'm going to kick into another gear' mode. Glad it didn't come to that."

Cairo's reaction to the gunfire was extreme, but he eventually overcame his aversion to become the first West Coast Navy SEAL canine warrior to be deployed. Lloyd and Cairo's pairing tells the story of the earliest days of the SEALs' use of canines and their training for a SOF environment. Those first efforts necessarily, were a case of expediency over experience. By that I mean that the command decided that the other SEAL teams should have access to the same "weapon," meaning MWDs, that SEAL Team Six had already been utilizing. However, there was no ready supply of dogs and trainers who could do the kinds of specific training that we do today. So the navy initially obtained a lot of its dogs from the civilian community. The closest thing that anyone had to the kind of dogs needed was "attack" dogs, as Lloyd called them, who worked for law enforcement agencies.

The vendors and trainers in those first few training classes had years of valuable experience providing and training dogs for the tasks required by civilian security forces. They weren't prepared to make these dogs the best possible partners to help SEALs carry out a mission-specific set of tasks. They didn't have the tactical experience. This isn't a knock on anyone, not the navy, not the breeders, the vendors, or the trainers. In fact, it was all just pretty much the way it is whenever something new starts up. You learn as you go and grow.

For Lloyd, being part of something new was enormously appealing. When word first came down that the SEALs were looking for volunteers, he was eager to get started with the program. A dog lover and not someone who adapted easily to a desk job, Lloyd saw this as the ideal opportunity for him. He had no formal experience in training dogs, but he wasn't alone in that. Actually, as a kind of blank slate, he was in some ways better off than someone who came into the program with preconceived ideas and habits that needed to be broken.

Lloyd soon realized he wasn't comfortable with all the training methods that were being used, but he followed the instructions he was given, trusting that what he was being told was the right thing. In order to correct the dogs, in those early days a correction stick, which was a cross between a riding crop and a billy club (a soft leather instrument), was used frequently. This is obviously not what you want to use if you're training a dog using positive reinforcement. Lloyd didn't like the idea of batting Cairo's snout with it, but it seemed to work. However, Lloyd is now pretty certain that Cairo's attack on him during the weapons-firing exercise wouldn't have happened if they'd been employing other training methods earlier on, in those days before I was involved with training.

"I knew that Cairo was a bit gun-shy, and he also saw me, because of how I was taught to correct him, as someone who caused him discomfort a lot of the time," Lloyd said, thinking back to that time. "Dogs are thinkers, but not on the most sophisticated level. He saw and heard me doing something he didn't like. He also saw me not so much as someone he didn't really like but someone he couldn't completely trust, and who, at times, he even feared. I was the source of most of his discomfort, so when the opportunity came along, and he was really uncomfortable and wanted to make the noise stop, he did what his breeding and his instincts told him to do—he came after me and tried to shut me down. I don't know exactly if rewarding him more during training would have helped us avoid that situation, but I think it would have."

Ironically, it was after that battle Lloyd and Cairo waged that their relationship changed significantly for the better. Perhaps they each sensed and respected the power of the other and decided it was best to work together as a team. It had been clear to Lloyd from their very first meeting that Cairo was a supreme alpha dog, but right from the start he knew, too, that the dog could be a calm presence.

"We weren't given a choice of which dog we were going to be paired off with," Lloyd recalled. "I was given a number and then told to go to the kennels and find the corresponding number. That was going to be my dog. I was also handed an ear-protection headphone-type device. Even with that on, the noise level in the kennel was incredible. My first response was to wonder what I had gotten myself into. I walked in there and these dogs were barking like mad. Some were chewing at the mesh in their kennel; a few were spinning around. It was pandemonium. When I got to my number, there was this dog just sitting there. He was high and tight, squared away like a good sailor, sitting there with his back straight, his head high, and his ears up. That's how he carried himself later, too, especially around the other dogs. He was very dominant, and I liked that about him."

In those early days of the program, the training facilities were not a part of any base. Training took place on the property of the breeder or trainer. The trainers believed that bonding with the dogs was important, so on that first day, the handler trainees took their dogs home. Actually, since they were far from their home bases, they took their dogs to nearby hotels. While the places allowed dogs, it's unlikely they were prepared for all these dogs and their handlers.

"We were all kind of surprised," recalled Lloyd, "that after just meeting these dogs for the first time and only going through some basic introductory information, filling out paperwork mostly, we were sent home with these clearly aggressive, high-energy dogs. We looked at each other and said, 'What are we supposed to do now?'"

The trainers had incorrectly assumed that Lloyd and the other members of this SEAL canine group had prior experience in handling working dogs. Lloyd vividly remembers those first few minutes in the hotel room. Cairo trotted in, using that high-stepping gait that the breed is known for. He sniffed around the room, checking out every corner of it. After a few minutes, he settled down on the floor, watchful but quiet.

"I got off easy," Lloyd said. "That night, in the room next to mine, I could hear this dog going crazy. It sounded like he was just chewing the place to pieces. I could hear things crashing to the floor. The next morning I asked the guy what was going on, and he told me that it wasn't as bad as what one of the other guys had gone through. After the dog tore up the room, that handler had put him in the car, figuring he could do less damage there. The dog ended up tearing up a headrest. He just chewed through the thing until all that was left of it was a metal frame and a pile of stuffing."

As time went on, Lloyd came to have a great deal of respect for Cairo's independent and fierce spirit. "He was tough. He wouldn't back down. A few simple corrections with the stick often weren't enough, he was that strong-willed. He knew what was right and wrong, but I think he sensed that I was new at this whole deal and he really tested me. As a result, I think in the end, he ended up teaching me much more than I taught him," Lloyd recalled.

Like most of the other handlers, Lloyd had had a successful naval career prior to joining the dog program. After graduating from BUD/S, his first assignment was with SEAL Delivery Vehicle Team (SDVT) One on the West Coast. The SDVT platoons are a subset of the SEAL teams and also fall under the Naval Special Warfare Command. They trace their origins back to World War II, when they worked with Italian and British combat swimmers, and their job is to deliver SEALs via submersibles to where they need to be to accomplish their mission, along with their equipment.

Lloyd also did a tour on the East Coast with SEAL Team Four, doing jungle work as well as participating in the effort to stop the flow of illegal drugs in South America. After two other assignments, and an opportunity he passed on to work with the navy's mammal program, he wound up exactly where he wanted to be—with Cairo.

During that first deployment in Iraq, every time Cairo assisted in a successful detection, the men in the platoon grew more and more comfortable with him. The detections might have been relatively small victories, but they emphasized that despite the large number of searches they had to do, every single one of them was important. As Cairo's find total increased, so did the men's belief in him and in the operation.

"Cairo was inspirational in a lot of ways," Lloyd recalled. "To see how tirelessly he went after it, running and searching night after night and day after day, you felt like you had to keep up with him. SEAL team members are a competitive bunch, and nobody wanted a dog to outdo them. Plus, just having him there, let alone when he made finds, was a huge morale boost. Maybe this is a bit of an exaggeration, but for me, even if Cairo hadn't had any finds or apprehensions, he would have been a valuable asset for us. Just having him there as a companion, one bit of home out there, was huge. And I don't mean just for me. Cairo was great with all the other team members. You're out there. You're hungry. You're tired. A dog comes up to you, and you feel better."

Lloyd and Cairo did a second rotation together, this one in Afghanistan, and the results were the same. As Lloyd said to me, "It's hard to prove a negative. By that I mean, how can you know how many lives those weapons and explosives might have taken if they'd been used? Since that didn't happen, we'll never really know. In my mind, that doesn't matter, the exact numbers."

Lloyd and Cairo are still together. Now that Cairo is retired, he enjoys his time off but needs to be worked fairly regularly. When he isn't doing some variation of his formal training, he still wants to be a working dog. "Cairo helps put the groceries away," Lloyd told me. "I hand him something, and for as powerful as those jaws are, when he carries a carton of milk or whatever, he never busts through the package. I was doing some work around the house, and I had a bunch of lumber delivered, and Cairo was helping out by dragging two-by-fours from the pile to where I was working. He wasn't about to just sit there and watch me. He also gets along well with my other two dogs, especially my little beagle. Cairo lets that little guy roll him. Cairo probably wouldn't like me telling people this, but he's got a thing for pillows—he just tears them up. He also has this little blanket that he carries around all the time. He's had it for years now, and I guess having it makes him feel secure."

Lloyd laughs at the irony of that statement. "He can still tear after things," he pointed out, "but I've never tried to see how he'd do in any drills with that blanket in his mouth."

13

SAMSON AND DAVE:
UNDETERRED UNDERDOGS

Kandahar, Afghanistan

There's an old saying that curiosity killed the cat. Well, in the case of one serviceman, his overly curious nature really annoyed a MWD named Samson. Samson and his handler, Dave, members of SEAL Team Three, were having their first meeting with the members of the platoon they were assigned to in Kandahar, Afghanistan. Dave did exactly what he'd been trained to do. He began by introducing himself and Samson to the assembled group of battle-tested men. He asked how many of them had served in a unit that was accompanied by a MWD. Just a few hands went up. When questioned further, those men revealed that the only dogs they'd seen had been sentry dogs back in the States. Having a dog with them in battle was a new experience.

The first thing Dave did after he finished his introductory remarks was to ask the members of the platoon to form a circle. He wanted them each to get a chance to handle Samson. This was designed to let them get comfortable with the Malinois and vice versa. He gave a detailed explanation of how the handoffs would go. He would bend down and pick up Samson, careful to wrap him up tightly in his arms, securing all four of the dog's legs. Only then would he hand the dog off to the next person in line. He reminded them that it was important that he take Samson back before the next soldier took his turn. That would be his way of communi-

cating to Samson that this was all okay. This would essentially be Dave telling the dog, "If Dad is handing you over to someone new, then you can and have to trust that new person, because I do."

Things went according to plan until an overeager soldier forgot about the handler-first rule. As soon as Samson was back on the ground, still in Dave's control, this guy bent down and put his face right next to Samson's. Then he tried to hug the dog to his chest in order to lift him up. Fortunately for everyone, Samson was on his best behavior. Instead of biting, he emitted a deeply guttural growl that let the soldier know that he didn't appreciate this guy not following the rules.

As Dave later told me, "That guy got off on the wrong foot with Samson, and Samson never forgot that breach of etiquette. Samson wasn't properly introduced to him; the guy overstepped his bounds, and from that point forward, whenever Samson saw the guy, he would growl."

Worse, the soldier in question professed to being a dog lover and was extremely interested in Samson and Dave and the training they'd undergone and other elements of the dog's life. Dave had to do his best to integrate himself into this group, and he didn't want to be rude. Also, he had told the guys that if they ever had any questions, he'd be happy to answer them. He just didn't anticipate how many questions this one guy would have.

After a few days of Samson getting to know everyone and adjusting to his new home, he wasn't always on leash while on the grounds of the FOB. Samson was friendly enough that he didn't pose a biting threat. He quickly proved to be a popular presence.

Several days after being attached to the team, Samson and Dave got word that they would be going out on a mission with the platoon. All the guys, including Dave, prepared early and left their gear outside where they were billeted. They would suit up at the last minute after their final briefings and take care of whatever personal business they had. Dave recalls walking out into a central area where piles of gear dotted the compound. He released Samson, who went to work immediately, nose to the ground, tail in the air, trying to locate any snacks. Or at least that was what Dave thought the dog was doing. Samson went from pile to pile and finally settled on one rucksack. He looked around, almost as if checking to see if anyone was watching him. Then he lifted his leg and let out a nice golden stream of urine on that rucksack. Dave felt bad, but what could he do? He stood to the side waiting to see who was the lucky owner of the soaking, smelly sack. You've probably already guessed who it was, and you're right. It was the impatient, overly curious serviceman. Dave isn't a malicious guy, but he had to laugh at his buddy Samson's way of getting his revenge.

Samson is a black-and-tan Malinois with an oversized head. It was that head, and the difference in color and size between it and body it was attached to, that caught Dave's attention the first time they met. Samson is small-framed, with a camel-colored torso and hindquarters, and a coal-black head and snout that in certain light makes his expressive eyes invisible. Dave admitted that this was not a case of love at first sight. "I'd seen all the other dogs," he said, "and then when Samson was assigned to me, I thought, *What? Why am I the one getting a dog that looks like it had been Frankenstein'd together from two other dogs?*' He was smaller than the dogs the rest of the guys in my training group were assigned, and that big head of his made him look like a buffalo or something. That image stuck, and eventually we all at one time or another thought of my big-skulled guy as Buffalo Head."

Dave's words sound harsher than they were. When we talked about Samson during one of my visits on behalf of my foundation, it was obvious the man has a deep affection for that dog. Dave and Samson spent two years serving several stints together in Afghanistan but are no longer working together.

"Samson has one more deployment scheduled," Dave told me. "He has to pass a physical before he can go back, and I hate to say this, but I hope he doesn't pass. Not that I want there to be something wrong with him, but I miss being with him. His new handler's a great guy, but Samson and I went through a lot together." Dave's voice trails off, and I can tell that Samson's enforced absence doesn't sit well with the dog's former partner.

I asked Dave about the last time he saw Samson. "You know, I had to be strong when we said good-bye. I couldn't get too worked up about it because of my wife and kids being there," said Dave. "If they saw me all down, then they would be even more upset. As it was, my wife was kind of torn up about it. He remembers me, though, of course, and the last time I went to visit him, he did his thing with me."

Dave described how Samson's ears pricked up as soon as he saw Dave. He then trotted toward him and thrust his head between Dave's legs so that his buddy could scratch him behind his ears. "Some dogs do that thing," Dave explained. "They press their heads up against you or between your legs. It's so cool that he does that. It's a very expressive gesture. It's like he's telling me that he's home. This is where he belongs. I asked some of the handlers and our trainers about that. They told me that this was his way of signaling that he knows that I've got his back and he's got mine. I've got kids, and I equate what Samson does with them coming up to me while I'm watching TV and hugging me or snuggling up against me. It's a very comforting feeling."

Dave knows that Samson is beginning to show some signs of wear and tear after his fairly intensive deployments. He's having digestive issues, and Dave thinks they're signs of stress. Dave worries about what might happen to Samson if he has to go back to Afghanistan one more time. "The dogs get it," Dave said. "They like to work, but they are surrounded by humans who are stressed out. They pick up on that and it affects them. It's just like if your house is a stressed-out place; even though you think you're doing your best to hide it, your whole family can sense it. So do the dogs when out in the field. The work is dangerous, and they do a great job when they're at it, but they have very little downtime."

Dave is eager for Samson to finish up his tests and either get deployed or retire. Either way—wait or not—Dave plans to adopt Samson and give him a good life when the dog finally retires.

How did these two manage to develop the deep bond they share when Dave was originally so skeptical about his canine partner? On a variation of another old saying, you can't judge a dog by the color of his fur or by the size of his head.

Dave and Samson share some qualities. It would have been easy to look at Dave's past and assume that he himself would be a less than ideal candidate for the SEALs, if you solely looked at the "what" of his life and not the "why" and "who" behind it. Dave was born in Brooklyn, New York, the son of a man who ran a small cleaning business that catered to local businesses. Dave didn't have the luxury of exploring his avid interest in sports—cross-country and baseball in particular. Shortly before he turned twelve years old, his mother left the family. Dave, his siblings, and his father lost a key source of income, but more importantly, Dave also lost her potentially positive influence and guidance. Dave had to leave school in 1987 at the age of fifteen to work, first with his father and later at a variety of other jobs. Dave had liked school, and while he hadn't been an outstanding student, his natural curiosity and sharp mind had helped him do well. He easily earned his GED, but work took precedence over everything else in his life.

"My dad had to work 24/7 to support us," Dave remembered. "That's just how it was. You do what you have to do. He had mouths to feed, but he couldn't do it on his own. I was the youngest, so I was the least far along in life is one way to put it. My older siblings, a brother and two sisters, were already pretty set on their life path when my mom left. They had to work hard, too, but they all got through high school, and each of them did some college work. That didn't seem like an option for me."

In the spirit of doing whatever it takes, Dave took a series of jobs for which he really wasn't eligible at his age. Eager to succeed, he altered his brother's driver's license to get a job at a pizza chain in Brooklyn. Within a year, at the age of seventeen, he was promoted to assistant manager. The work wasn't the most rewarding or challenging, but the money helped. Dave's dreams back then mostly revolved around muscle cars—a 1969 Nova and a 1971 Camaro that he worked on—but the streets of Brooklyn held other allures besides fast cars. Street gangs, drugs, and petty crime influenced many of Dave's peers. A few turned hardcore, but most were just directionless kids with no real idea where they wanted to go or who they wanted to be. Dave put himself in that category, though his work ethic kept him from ever sliding too far down into anything like the serious thug life.

By the time he was twenty, he realized that a career in the fast-food world was, for him, a long drive down a boring stretch of highway that led to no place interesting. He enrolled in community college, took a few courses, and then lost interest. This pattern repeated itself more than once.

Finally, a friend told him that he should consider life in the military as a way out and told him about the SEALs. Having a brother who had served, and seeing little in the way of options based on what he'd seen of his friends and peers on the street, Dave's curiosity was piqued. More than that, Dave realized that making the SEAL teams would be a real challenge, and Dave felt he was up for it. He'd spent most of his young adult life trying to escape the idea of being the "baby brother." He wanted to make that transition from being a kid to being a man. About the most seriously illegal thing he'd done was get a job using a fake ID, but he saw even that as a positive. He had found a way to get a mission accomplished. He figured that attitude would serve him well. One day he headed over to a local recruitment office.

"I walked in the place," Dave recalled, "and the first office was for the marines. I'd started to have some doubts about the SEALs. They were the elite and all, and I wondered if I could cut it. So I walked toward the open door, and this marine staff sergeant looked me up and down and this weird kind of smile passed over his face. Then he got serious for a second and yelled out, 'Halt! Stop where you're at. I want you to do an about-face.'

"I stood there staring at the guy, wondering, *What is this guy talking about, about-face?* Before I could say anything, he walked out of this office, saying, again in this loud, shrill voice, 'Think about the rest of your life, and then come back in here.'

"I said to him, 'What? Excuse me?'

" 'You heard me,' he said. 'Turn around. Get out of here. Think about what you're about to do and then come back.'

"I stood there shaking my head, trying to figure out what this guy's deal was. Out of the corner of my eye, I saw two other men in uniform, from the navy. They were seated at desks, and a glass partition separated them from this marine and me. They were both smiling and laughing a bit, and then a navy recruiter stood up, walked over to his door, stuck his head out, and said, 'Dude, why don't you come on in here?' "

This guy sounded like somebody Dave could better relate to, so he went in. After a couple of introductory exchanges, Dave mentioned his interest in the SEALs and signed up for the navy.

Unfortunately, that recruiter didn't sign Dave up for the Dive Farer program. Dive Farer was a way for the navy to identify potential candidates for the SEAL teams. They do additional training beyond what the rest of the recruits do. Dave assumed that when he got to boot camp, he'd be with the Dive Farer candidates, but when the group was to formally muster, his name wasn't called. Dave went to his basic training instructor and asked about the omission. There's an old story going around that some recruiters for the armed forces tell potential candidates anything they want to hear to get them to sign up. This sure looked like one of those cases.

The instructor looked at his list and then at Dave. "Let me guess," he said. "Your recruiter told you you were going to be a SEAL?"

Dave nodded.

The recruiter shook his head, "No. He got you," he said. "You're going to a big, old, gray ship when you're done here."

Following basic training in 1992, Dave was assigned a Machine Repair rating and put to work. At first he was looking for a way to get out, but he was told that he'd made a four-year commitment.

Dave decided that he was going to have to learn to live with his situation. He also learned that no tricks had been played on him. The recruiter had said that he *could* qualify for the SEALs. Dave had passed the initial physical fitness qualifier, but he hadn't scored high enough on a written test to make the first cut. In high school, before he'd dropped out, he'd taken the Armed Services Vocational Aptitude Battery. His score on that had been his undoing.

"That was another time when I could only do what I knew best," Dave said. "Work as hard as I could to prove that I could get things done." He proved to be a hustler in the most positive sense. "Being an engineman wasn't my idea of making it to the top and proving myself," he said. "I figured that if I had to do my time, I'd take full advantage of every opportunity I had."

That attitude translated into taking as many courses as he could, earning citations for exemplary work, and doing everything he could to stand out, in a positive way, from the rest of his shipmates. He picked his shots, but he let his superiors know that he was still interested in going to BUD/S. His plan worked. When told that if he made the next rank he'd get his shot, he made sure that it happened. It took three years to get to BUD/S, and when he did, he made the most of that chance, too.

Prior to entering the canine program to become a handler, Dave served for a total of thirteen years. He was deployed to both Iraq and Afghanistan. When he started to work with Samson, Dave realized that the two of them had been wrongly prejudged— Dave by that marine recruiter who years ago had taken him for a typical kid off the street, and Samson when everyone thought the striking contrast between his slight frame and his oversized head made him look like a less than ideal MWD. Actually, Samson's head was a slight advantage. Remember that study done on dogs' jaws to determine bite strength? It showed that the longer the jaw and the broader the skull, the greater the pressure a dog could exert. Hello, Samson.

Like a lot of the other handlers, as a kid, Dave had dogs as pets. His family had a series of dogs, but the ones he remembers most fondly were the Rottweilers. From the beginning, Dave paid close attention to the dogs, and he learned a lot from doing this. He was able to tell that a dog had different barks for different situations. He learned that his dogs barked one way when a stranger was coming to the door and another way when a family member was approaching. Dave laughed when he told me how this knowledge came in handy: The dogs served as early warning devices for him and his siblings. If the dogs' bark alerted them that their parents were coming, the kids knew they had to immediately stop doing anything they shouldn't be doing before their mom and pop came through the front door.

He saw the dogs as the younger siblings that he didn't have, and coming home from school to a dog's greeting and attention helped to ease the pain he felt at his mother's departure. The dogs also helped to fill the void he felt when his older brother and sisters left home. One dog in particular, Rebecca von Hufning, a female Rottie, filled that void particularly well.

Dave took her for long walks and although he had no real idea of how to formally train a dog, he made his own efforts at it. He became such a regular in the neighborhood walking the Rottie that at one point a man who was out walking another Rottweiler approached him. The man was about to go to prison, and he wanted to be sure that his beloved dog would be well cared for. He offered Dave the dog, and Dave accepted. His father wasn't too pleased with the idea of having another canine mouth to feed, and sometimes he used the threat of expelling the dogs from the house to get Dave to do what was asked of him. Father and son had some tension between them, but the threat was never made real.

Dave's love of dogs made him an ideal candidate to become a SEAL team dog handler. His interest in dogs also made it easy for him to follow one of the key training mantras we have, which is "Watch your dog every minute so that you know him better than you've known anybody." Dave was a keen observer, and by watching Samson carefully he was very quickly able to figure out what his dog was thinking and feeling. Early on, for instance, he noticed how Samson interacted with other dogs, particularly ones that he didn't like. "If he doesn't like a dog," Dave said, "he'll shake his tail and wave it back and forth three or four times and stop. Then three or four times more and stop; three or four times and stop. He is almost luring the other dog in, because when a dog wags his tail, he's letting another dog know that he's friendly and that everything's okay. Samson kind of disguises his real intention, which is to growl up in that other dog's face."

Handlers need to be extremely familiar not just with all the traits and habits of their dogs, but with their bodies, too. It's all critically important, because a dog can't tell you with words when he's not feeling his best physically or mentally. A handler has to be able to detect when a dog is ill, has been worked too hard, or has developed some negative association with some phase of an operation. If a dog is not working to full capacity, that's like a soldier being distracted by events back home, like a weapon that hasn't been maintained properly and might misfire, or like a piece of communications equipment that has been overused or somehow damaged. All those things become a liability.

An important thing to remember about these dogs is that because they are bred and trained at such a high level, like any supremely competitive athlete, they want to be in the game all the time, despite how they may feel. The signs of a dog not performing at 100 percent are often subtle. The years a handler and a dog spend in training and developing a bond help the handler become familiar with his dog to the degree that he can spot almost any minor fluctuations in health or behavior.

Anyone who's ever owned a dog knows that they are "creatures of habit." Any break from their normal pattern of behavior is something that a handler has to investigate. Ironically, that kind of scrutiny is something that is also essential in warfare. Soldiers are trained and develop habits, and they are trained to identify the habits and routines of their enemies and to notice any breaks in them. Similarly, they are trained to look for anything unusual in their environment. That constant examination and evaluation of what is usual and what is unusual is one of the fundamental elements of modern warfare, and it has been practiced in recent years in fighting insurgencies in both urban and nonurban environments.

— —

Samson excels at detection work, and Dave discovered that one of Samson's most interesting and extremely useful abilities is one that he shares with a lot of other dogs doing detection work. They have the ability to detect the odor of something that isn't there. During multiple operations in Afghanistan, Samson had gone into places and detected explosives when there were none to be found. It may sound like his nose was "off" and that he failed, but that always turned out not to be the case. Instead, each time interpreters working with the United States questioned cooperating Afghani civilians in the area, they found out that Samson had discovered a site that the Taliban had recently used to make explosives, or he had detected a location where there had been an IED that had since been moved. Samson's nose was right on the money. He detected residue and remnant odors, and the teams were able to note the locations. This helped them to plot the Taliban's movement and to detect patterns and, subsequently, variations from those patterns.

— —

In June and July, the average daily temperature in Kandahar is 102.2°F (39°C). The nighttime low averages 66°F (19°C). Those nighttime cool temperatures plus the cover of darkness make late-night operations in some ways ideal and in others anything but. The operational tempo during a deployment can be dictated by the frequency of missions but also by their irregular nature. Anyone who works an irregular schedule that is a mix of daytime and nighttime hours can attest to the toll that takes after a while.

Dave and Samson were on their second deployment. They had both clearly learned some things their first time in country. The high operational tempo during their first deployment had been tough on them both; participating in nightly missions for weeks on end had put a strain on them. Toward the end of that first six-month deployment, Dave noticed that Samson wasn't eating with his usual gusto and was having some digestive issues. Samson eventually became his usual self again, and by the time of their second deployment, Dave was satisfied that Samson was at the top of his game both physically and mentally. He was still observing Samson intently and was glad that even though they were in a particularly hot zone in terms of engagements with the enemy, Samson seemed little worse for wear halfway through the duration of their assignment.

The intense heat played a significant part in Dave's concern about Samson's well-being and his performance capability, as did the operational tempo and the irregular schedule of the missions. In addition, the members of this team were also working to train the Host Nation Security Forces in Afghanistan so the Afghan military could function with a higher degree of efficiency to defend their own country against insurgencies.

One very hot and very bright day in July 2010, Dave and Samson were doing explosive-detection work on a heavily traveled road northwest of Kandahar. The road was one used by both troops and civilians. Dave recalls the ride out from Kandahar. "We all piled into the back of a Toyota HiLux pickup," he said, "a vehicle you see just about everywhere over there. Samson was in good spirits. We set out just as the sun was coming up, so it was still comfortable. As hard as it is to think of a place like that being beautiful, it's so dry and the scrub brush and desert are so brown and tan, at that hour, the early morning sunlight softened everything. We passed a few small villages, just a few low-slung houses.

"Like any dog, Samson liked driving along, scenting the air. He was always comfortable in vehicles, and this ride was no exception. He was cool with being with me and the other team members, and he showed no sign that the Host Nation dudes were any different to him. It was hard to tell how they felt about Samson. They mostly just ignored him."

After an hour or more of driving, they stopped at a checkpoint. Dave and Samson both took a good long drink before getting started. They were to clear a stretch of road about a mile and a half long. After they finished, the other members of the team would follow up and do a routine patrol.

"In introducing Samson to the other members of the team, I'd had to let them know what his limits were," Dave recalled. "Some of the guys were surprised that he'd 'only' be able to do a certain distance at a time. They looked at the kind of shape he was in and thought that he could go for miles and miles. And in certain instances, he can. I had to explain that in training, covering that kind of distance was no problem—if he wasn't in continuous search mode. Just trotting along or even sprinting two and a half miles was nothing for him. I explained that when he was on detection continuously, his breathing was different. I tried to get them to imagine what it would be like for them to run while exhaling and inhaling about one revolution per second. That's what Samson would have to do, all the time taking in the dust from these dirt roads."

Once Samson and Dave began their first portion of the detection work, another issue came up. "The winds were swirling and crisscrossing all over the place," he said, "so that meant we had to be quartering the wind [moving at an angle instead of straight into it] from left to right. Samson was on leash, and we headed along the right-hand side of the road, with him doing his serpentine tracking. After all the training we'd done and all the experience he had in the field, I didn't have to lead Samson to the downwind side. He just knew where to go."

Two other team members were on comms, and they had air support from above; an AC-130 gunship was serving as their eyes in the sky.

After an hour, they stopped for a break. Dave waited for Samson's respiration rate to slow. How much of his panting was due to the rising temperature and his exertion level was something that Dave had to figure out. He didn't want to work Samson too hard and didn't want the dog to get overheated. Though Malinois naturally shed their undercoats in hot weather, Samson still had a thick top coat, and his black head absorbed the sun's rays in the way a lighter color wouldn't. Dave knew the dog had to feel a lot hotter than the humans in their gear.

Dave led Samson back to the truck. The Host Nation trainees needed some more practice, so they clambered out of the truck and started doing their own search with a detection machine. After a few minutes, Dave could hear some excited talking.

"They thought they'd hit on something," he recalled. "They started digging around a bit, but it turned out that there was nothing there. Their machine must have hit on something, but it wasn't a trigger or a device."

While the Host Nation guys continued to explore what they thought was a hot area, Dave led Samson up ahead so the dog could relieve himself. Dave expected Samson to stop somewhere to do his business. Samson did stop, but not to do the kind of business that Dave expected.

"We were a hundred or so yards ahead of the Host Nation soldiers," said Dave, "and I saw Samson's ears go straight up. I knew he was on something, but at that point, it could have been anything he might have seen or smelled. Then his tail went high and he wagged it. That's when I thought that he was on some explosives. When he detects human odor, it's the low wag. Explosive stuff, high tail wags. That's Samson's 'tell.' Other dogs I know, one of them tucks his tail in, another poops. They've all got their way of letting you know they're on something. This time, though, it was just one quick high tail wag and he stopped. I figured it was nothing, and I turned around to go back to the truck. Samson followed for a second, but then he turned back and did it again. Then he seemed to lose it again. I was getting worried, thinking that maybe something was wrong with him, that maybe all the heat and stress was too much."

After Samson gave another hit signal and showed another few signs of uncertainty, Dave knew what to do. "I know that the dogs, when on leash, sometimes don't signal as strongly and surely as they would off leash," he explained. "Something about their instincts makes them better at detection on their own. So I released him. Good thing I did."

About 40 yards from where Samson had first showed indications that he'd hit on an explosive odor, he sat on the spot. Dave called Samson back to him, and the men proceeded to use one of the machines to verify that Samson had indeed found something; it turned out to be a trigger switch. Another one was just a few yards away. The IED itself was wired and waiting on the opposite side of the road.

"That was a big find," said Dave. "The EOD detail followed up and said that the IED was too large to transport and destroy. After we finished they came back and exploded it. I can't talk about the specifics of what we found, but an IED that large would have done some major damage to us or whoever else came across and detonated it."

As soon as Samson returned to his side, Dave rewarded him. "I gave him his tennis ball and played with him for a few minutes, and then gave him a couple of dog treats I carry with me," he said. "Samson seemed pretty happy to just have those."

For a dog whose head-to-body ratio and slight build were the source of much teasing, Samson sure had turned into a battle-tested detection expert. Samson just does the job that SOF dogs do, but the dog also has a soft side that is perhaps best illustrated by another story Dave told.

"We were back on shore leave," Dave recalled, "and were out and about. This woman in front of us was pushing her kid in a stroller. We were behind them and saw the kid drop a stuffed animal. When we got up to it, I could see that it was Elmo from *Ses-*

ame Street. Samson picked it up, and he did that usual dog thing of kind of strutting proudly with his 'look what I found' head-high thing going on. I hurried a bit to catch up to the woman, and she heard us coming and turned around. Her eyes got all big and she instinctively stepped in front of her baby to protect him.

"We put the brakes on. The lady was looking at Samson and the toy he had in his mouth, and I could tell she was not happy. I started to apologize, but then she kind of smiled a bit. I told Samson to release, and he did immediately. The woman's smile widened. She nodded her head. After that she said, 'Let him keep it. That's the least I can do. That dog's out there saving lives.' I knew she was familiar with our program, living nearby and all. I thanked her. Well, Samson loves that toy. He never tore it up. I've still got it. When he comes back and I get to keep him when he retires, that toy will be right here waiting for him. I can't wait to see his reaction."

14

REX AND DWAYNE:
FOILING INSURGENTS

Afghanistan

It had a been another long, exhausting day in a string of eight- to twelve-hour days Rex and his handler, Dwayne, had spent on the move with the EOD guy and point man, searching fields, wells, and buildings for explosives, while most of the rest of the SEAL team took up security positions. As the sun angled lower in the sky, a call came over the radio that another suspicious area needed to be searched, yet one more walled compound. From the outside, this compound seemed no different from any of the hundreds they'd previously gone through. Once Dwayne and Rex entered the compound, however, they immediately saw not only a small roofed structure where livestock was being kept but, sitting along the far wall, a dozen or more Afghan civilians.

Gaunt, with concave cheeks behind their beards, their eyes large beneath their brimless, short, round kufi caps, the men sat there in the dust. Their stained and tattered shalwar kameez—pants and tunic—fluttered in the breeze. Dwayne asked his teammates to clear out the animals. There was a smelly assortment of goats and a few sheep, all of whom expressed indifference to their orders to disperse. They were all also reluctant to go near Rex, whose agitation and desire were evident in his barking and straining at his leash. Dwayne took Rex a relatively safe distance away, still within the walls, and waited.

"Even though the animals were finally led out, their stench was still there," Dwayne recalled. *"The sound of the buzzing flies was nearly loud enough to make any conversation difficult. Rex searched, and he made a solid find—blasting caps and a large quantity of other IED-making materials. It took him a few trips, but the EOD guy took them all out of there, while Rex and I stood by. At that point, it would have been easy to just be a spectator. Rex had done his job. I'd played tug with him to reward him, and a couple of other guys came by to pet him. I figured, though, that if there was that much explosive material here, then maybe there were other things around."*

Dwayne led Rex on a search around the perimeter. About a minute into it, Rex got a whiff of something, and he started tugging Dwayne. He went straight toward those seated men, who were now being detained under suspicion of being part of the Taliban. *"I was thinking maybe he was interested in them,"* Dwayne told me, *"but he stopped just short of them. In front of where the prisoners were, there was a sea buckthorn bush. Those bushes have plenty of seriously sharp, sharp thorns. Rex indicated on that and sat down looking at it."*

Dwayne cautiously looked for himself, but the bush's heavy concentration of leaves and thorns made it nearly impenetrable. So he got the EOD guy to come over. Dwayne noted that the Afghanis being held were starting to get restless.

Two fully loaded AK-47s were found right under the bush, just outside arm's reach of the suspected Taliban members. All those men would have had to do was time a quick scramble and the operation could have turned into a very bad incident.

——

It was obvious that the guns had been placed there as part of some larger plan. How much Rex's presence, and the Afghanis' reluctance to mess with him, played into how that threat was neutralized wasn't clear. What was obvious was that Rex's ability to detect those weapons foiled the enemy's plans.

"That was my proudest moment working with Rex," Dwayne told me as he recalled the incident. "In my mind, he saved a lot of our lives that day."

When the operation was concluded and they returned to the FOB, Dwayne followed his usual routine. He went to the chow hall, which was really little more than a small room with a few tables, and had Rex lie down along a far wall. "Rex is like most dogs," said Dwayne. "He loves to eat; I had to always be careful to keep his weight down. He got his meals, and a few treats. The one thing I was insistent on with the guys was that they not give him any junk food.

"At the FOB we had a 'theater,' another small room with a TV, where we could watch movies. There were some chairs and a couch, and Rex always hung out with us in there. I never had to muzzle him because he was so friendly. After that great find that day, I knew I had to be even more vigilant than normal with the guys to make sure they didn't get lax and give him anything that would be bad for him in the long run. I knew they were grateful for what he'd done, but still."

Dwayne rewarded Rex, as he always did after a meal, for staying at his "post." He brought him a couple of bites of meat, in this case chicken. Later that night Rex did his usual thing. While the movie was on, he climbed onto the couch with a couple of the team members to get as comfortable as possible. He slept for a bit, woke up, and walked around the room looking for attention. Not that he needed to ask for it.

"If it weren't for the fact that we were in an FOB in Afghanistan, you could almost imagine yourself back at home in a rec room or basement or whatever, hanging out with your buddies watching a movie," Dwayne said. "Your dog was doing his best to mooch a treat but settled for a few ear and belly scratches. He'd get blamed for a few odors that were worse than those in that livestock pen, but that's just boys being boys."

— ·—

Rex's success at his job and his easy camaraderie with the human members of the team were many miles away from where he had started as an MWD, and not just geographically speaking. Rex had, in a way, been a black sheep among the new trainee dogs. He had been sitting in a kennel, mostly untrained, for a year when he was paired with Dwayne. Rex was "green"; he was an inexperienced and unrefined dog that hadn't been trained in any of the dog sports and didn't have a firmly established foundation in obedience either. "Rex's big problem," recounted Dwayne, "was his refusal to give up his toy. Getting a dog to release something is pretty essential. Rex thought it was kind of a game, and he was better at it than the rest of us. When we tried to trick him into giving the ball back, he always outsmarted us. It was like he had a perimeter-limit warning device—he'd let you in only so close before he'd dart away. Or he'd just sit there turning his head away so that you couldn't get the ball out of his mouth. Smart dog, but frustrating.

"The first thing I remember about Rex, though, was that he didn't look like any German shepherd dog I'd ever seen before," Dwayne told me. "I did my research and found out that the breeding lines and what was considered proper conformation/makeup of the dog's body had changed since the 1950s. Rex looked like a classic German shepherd from the 1940s. He has a really big head and large paws and a very straight back. The dogs bred from the newer lines generally have smaller paws and heads, and they also have more of a swayed back. It's just my opinion, but that classic look— the lines of dogs like Rex are just much more beautiful."

Like some of the other handlers in the then-new dog handling program, Dwayne didn't like some of the methods, but he had to do what he was being trained to do. "Choking a dog off a toy isn't a good idea," he said. "It creates resentment in the dog, and distrust. After you do that a few times, every time you approach the dog, he's going to think that you want to choke him off that toy. All you're doing is reinforcing that drive to hang on to what I've got." Dwayne noticed an instructor/trainer who was observing from the sidelines as they put the dogs through their routine in the basic handler course. "Every time we used the collar on the dogs, to choke him off the bite or anything else, I'd look over and see that man shaking his head," he recalled. "I went over to him a few times to get his take on things. He was pretty highly regarded in Germany, and he just said that our use of compelling the dogs to do what we wanted, instead of encouraging or rewarding the dogs, was just making some things worse."

Dwayne learned more and more about positive reinforcement and the importance of timing a correction or a reward as the program went along. "That reward has to be instantaneous. Bonding with a dog is all about the dog learning to trust you. If you get a dog to the point where he knows you have his best interests in mind, and you do that enough times in different situations, you earn some credit with that dog," he explained. "It's just like with humans. You have to earn someone's trust. What we might call treating a dog with dignity and love translates in their minds to one thing—trust. Start with the small things and work your way up the scale."

Similarly, Dwayne learned that as far as ability to detect odors is concerned, a dog can start big and break things down into very small parts. "When you're a SEAL, you learn about explosives from one perspective. I'm simplifying, of course, but basically we learn how to use them," he explained. "We rely on the dogs for detection, and one of the things that surprised me was that the amount of an explosive being used can sometimes confuse a dog. A dog's nose is so sensitive that—let's say 50 grams of RDX or other explosive ordnance are being used in training. Well, a ton of RDX is going to smell different to a dog than that small sample will. So, in training, we have to work at exposing the dogs to varying concentrations so that they won't be confused. The thing is that RDX is the major ingredient in C-4, so if your dog can detect RDX, he is going to be able to pick up C-4, because that's essentially 94 percent RDX plus some plasticizers and fillers.

"What was made clear to me is that we as humans can walk into our kitchen and smell beef stew cooking. We may be able to pick up traces of the ingredients in that stew, but for a dog that stew's odor is immediately broken down into its component parts—beef, potato, carrots, onion, and whatever else is in there," said Dwayne.

"That's why efforts to disguise drugs or explosives or whatever with masking odors don't work. A dog can pick out all the individual components of any odor."

➡ ➖

Most of what Dwayne knows about dogs he learned from his exposure to them while in the service. His family had a Pekingese while he was growing up, and according to Dwayne, while he was a fine dog, he just wasn't the kind of dog with whom Dwayne personally bonded. He remembers his first exposure to working dogs took place when bomb-detection dogs from civilian contractors were assigned to his military unit. "I'd never seen a Dutch Shepherd or a Malinois before," he recalled," and I just thought they were the most incredible-looking dogs."

It was years before Dave began working with the dog handler program. He was originally drawn to the navy because he loved the ocean and diving. At fifteen, he began an open-water PADI (Professional Association of Diving Instructors) program when he was staying with his father for the summer in the mountains near Santa Cruz. Scheduling conflicts prevented him from making the last open-water dive, so he didn't get certified. "I was definitely disappointed at not being able to follow through to the end," he told me, "but the really funny thing is that I was a terrible swimmer. My parents had the hardest time teaching me. I got to the point where I could just get by in the pool, but there was something about being under the water."

He took up diving when he attended a private school, where for a six-week period, as part of an enrichment program, students were encouraged to pursue an interest. Dwayne chose diving and once again took a certification course, and once again he failed to complete it. He also didn't finish his education at that private school.

"I got kicked out," he admitted. "I was one of those classic 'does not apply himself' types. Looking back on it now, failing to finish those first two dive programs was typical of how I approached a lot of things. I'd start something, get all fired up about it, lose interest, and then move on to something else. But those failures were more like delays. Those interests didn't just die out completely, they'd end up in the back of my mind, and eventually I'd get around to finishing what I'd started."

Dwayne was one of the fortunate few whose navy recruiter seemed to recognize something in him. Dwayne had never heard of the SEALs, but his recruiter mentioned them to him because Dwayne had expressed an interest in getting certified as a diver, hoping that the third time would be the charm.

"I was so clueless about the SEALs," Dwayne said with a laugh, "that I asked the guy, 'Do they do any kind of diving?' He just looked at me and said, 'Yes. They do.' Then I asked him if the training for the SEALs was hard. Again I got a kind of puzzled look, and the recruiter kind of stuck to his script. 'No. Not really.' Then they showed me the video, and it looked like what the SEAL team members were doing was a lot of fun. I think I even said those exact words to the guys in the enlistment office.

"But the good thing was, I enlisted and was a part of the Dive Farer program," he went on. "I did my basic training in Florida and then went on to Millington, Tennessee, for my A school. From A school, I went straight to BUD/S. That was an eye-opener."

Dwayne was a good student of human nature. "I developed a game plan right away once I realized how tough this was going to be," he told me. "I saw some of these guys; they looked like chiseled Greek god statues, and a whole bunch of the others gravitated toward them. They all projected this attitude—arrogance, I guess, is the best word to describe it—and I just didn't want to be a part of that. I wasn't a 'Mister Popular' type guy; I wasn't a hero worshipper either. The thing is, when those studs fell by the wayside, so did their followers eventually. They saw their leader go down, and they must have thought that if this guy I admire so much couldn't handle it, then how can I possibly do it? In a way, my being a kind of loner type paid off for me."

Despite Dwayne's early habit of not finishing what he started, he did graduate from BUD/S in class 180 in 1991. He was then assigned to a SEAL team. He felt he had a bit of bad timing. "There wasn't any real combat in the world at that time," he recalled. "I just missed the Gulf War. The last platoon heading into that theater left a month or two before I graduated. Our first workups were in Southeast Asia to do Foreign Internal Defense assignments. That was okay, doing that kind of teaching and goodwill work. At least it wasn't all the same, since we'd lead dive courses, some segment pair operations, and some jumps. The best part was Cobra Gold (annual training exercises in Thailand). But I don't know anybody who graduated from BUD/S and didn't want to put all their training to use as an operator."

Dwayne moved on to become a sniper and later a sniper instructor. He went to language school to learn Thai, then went on another deployment out of Guam doing more FID work. In 2000, he volunteered to become a free-fall instructor. A great need for those instructors existed, so Dwayne "jumped" at the chance. Once qualified as an instructor, he taught SOF and other Department of Defense candidates the fine skills needed to use nonstandard parachute equipment. He spent the next three years in Yuma, Arizona, doing that work. Next, he rejoined a SEAL team and started working up to go to Iraq. Once deployed in Iraq, he served as a member of a security detail protecting high-level Iraqi government officials. That was where he met those bomb-sniffing working dogs that made such a powerful impact on him.

However, because the need for free-fall instructors still existed, Dwayne returned to Yuma. Finally, in 2008, he changed assignments, working for Support Activity One, a unit that deals with high-security-clearance intelligence. That job proved to be more administrative than Dwayne would have liked.

"Being behind a desk and dealing with all kinds of written reports wasn't working out too well for me," he recounted. "Intelligence work is important, but it's definitely not that active an assignment. Definitely not a James Bond experience. In fact, I felt like the relative inactivity was draining the life out of me. The command had just acquired the multipurpose canine unit from NSW Group One, and I was asked if I had any interest in going over there because they were shorthanded. I thought to myself that program was just about my speed. I think I have the attention span equal to a dog's, so why not? I loved being outdoors, and this desk wasn't a good fit."

Dwayne sure got what he wished for when he opted to get out from sitting behind a desk. He and the other handler trainees and their dogs were taken all over the country to train in different environments. The theory was that the more you sweat in training, the less you bleed in the war. So they traveled to deserts, places like the jungle, urban environments, and high elevations. Frequently they went to heavily populated skiing areas and traveled up to an elevation of 10,000 feet with 4 feet of snow on the ground. They practiced explosive-detection work under those conditions. Humidity, barometric pressure, wind, altitude, snow cover—all of these things affect how explosive odor travels, how much of it spreads. A dog may be able to find any odor you want in a regular and familiar environment, but when you take him to 10,000 feet and bury an odor under 4 feet of snow, that's a completely different ball game.

Dwayne and Rex did all that, but even those extremes and the incredible amount of training they had to do didn't fully prepare them for the rigors of their deployment to Afghanistan. However, the actual getting to Afghanistan was pretty easy. Rex couldn't fly in the cargo hold of the commercial flight taking them overseas. So he got to fly coach, sitting at Dwayne's feet the whole time, very content. This was a new experience for Rex, and when he stayed calm Dwayne rewarded him. A few passengers even came up to greet him, and Dwayne let them.

Once in Afghanistan's Zabul Province, however, even though the two weren't deployed to the mountainous regions—approximately 40 percent of the land—the landscape they were in and the work they were doing were still intense.

Their SEAL team engaged in a number of firefights against

the Taliban on that deployment and covered a large operational sector within the province. Even though the men and Rex weren't actively engaged in clearing operations the entire time they were away from the FOB, those three- to four-hour rides on rutted tracks that wouldn't fit any definition of roads added to the fatiguing nature of the job they were doing. Like all other handlers, Dwayne had to be vigilant about his dog's condition.

"You start to wonder if your dog is going to break down, not in the mental sense necessarily, but physically also. This was his first tour of duty, this was my first time with him, all of this was new, and so you become hyperaware. You have to be. I would give him rests, and I'd also make sure that he stayed hydrated at all times," Dwayne told me. "On the mental side, we'd go for long periods where he wouldn't make any hits, and that was hard on him. He wanted that reward; he wanted to succeed. To keep his spirits up, to keep him as motivated as could be, I'd frequently plant objects for him to find. That way I was keeping that reward in the front of his mind all the time."

Functioning as part of the team and respecting roles and responsibilities is important on a deployment. Because of Rex's detection and apprehension work, he and Dwayne had to walk point, ahead of their unit. "Even though we walk point, that doesn't mean that we take on the full responsibilities of the point man," Dwayne explained. "Point man's a prestigious job, and guys wouldn't like it if you came in there and just acted like you were taking over. I told them that my job with Rex was to make sure they didn't walk over any IEDs. They were still responsible for navigating the route and making all the decisions that go along with that. I often looked back at that point guy and keyed off what he was indicating to me. The only time I would divert them from a route was if Rex detected something or showed early indicators that he was on explosive odor.

"From the very beginning, we have it drummed into our heads that as much as we're out there fighting a war or trying to take out bad guys, we're really looking out for one another," said Dwayne.

"When you're in combat like we were, that becomes even more clear, if such a thing's possible. All the other stuff, the politics of the war and whatnot, how the Host Nation civilians feel about our being there, that goes away. I'm there to save my teammates and myself."

Very early in their deployment, Rex did something that earned the trust of the other SEAL team members. The region they were assigned to was primarily made up of agricultural fields, where the main crop was pistachio nuts. The team was in a fairly broad and flat valley, and the region was dotted with grape arbors. "I don't know much about wine, but apparently extremes of temperatures are good for the grapes," said Dwayne. "It was 110°F to 120°F during the day, and then at night, at that elevation, it dropped by 30°F to 40°F. We came on one fairly large vineyard, something I didn't expect to see in Afghanistan, and a call came over the comms that Rex and I needed to check something out. A drying hut, one of the larger structures in the area, that was maybe 65 feet high, a stone building with gaps at the top for ventilation, needed to be checked out."

The interior of the drying hut was essentially one large room with a few pieces of framing-type lumber serving as partitions. Given the building's size, roughly 750 square feet, Rex had a fairly significant amount of ground to cover, especially after a day in which he'd already covered more than 6 miles (not all of which was spent, strictly speaking, in detection work). The search came up empty. As they were exiting the building and about to rejoin the rest of the members of the team, Rex, as Dwayne put it, "keyed up on something," and he started pulling him. They came to a motorbike, a small single-cylinder thing that looked about the size of a moped. It was all beat up; the engine cases were crusted with oil and dirt, and the metal had a yellowish patina from gas leaking onto it and drying there. "I could only imagine what it smelled like to Rex, because the thing reeked of all those odors in *my* nose," Dwayne remembered. "But he made a strong indication on that bike, and he sat next to it, letting me know he'd found something."

Dwayne saw a small package under the frame's top tube that supported the gas tank and the seat. He called the EOD guy over, who normally walked right alongside him and the dog. "He wanded it, and then the point man came up behind us. We could all see something was there. The EOD man got the package out of there, and he discovered a dozen or so rounds of ammo," Dwayne explained. "The package was wrapped up in feet and feet of something like duct tape. It was all wound into this very intricate pattern, almost like it was woven. Obviously, whoever had done that didn't want to have ready access to it, but they also really didn't want anybody else to know what was in there. In terms of its potential threat to our safety, that package posed minimal danger. Sure, those rounds could have been used against us, but nothing was rigged to explode."

The important and somewhat impressive part of this is that at a distance of more than 100 yards, through a mixed-odor vapor of petroleum and gasoline, and shifting winds and swirling dust and packing that may or may not have been designed to contain that explosive odor, Rex had discovered it. In the early days of deployment of Navy SEAL dogs, this was very good work. As someone who's very experienced in working with the kinds of multipurpose dogs the SEALs use, I wouldn't get knocked off my chair by news like that if it happened today. Sure, I'd be pleased, but my more measured response would be due to the fact that I've seen and experienced much more. That's not to take anything away from the work Rex did that day. It was important, and sometimes timing is everything.

The other members of the SEAL team were impressed by Rex's find, and as Dwayne recalled, it helped him earn his credibility with the team.

— • —

Rex was only deployed that one time. A change in trainers and protocols meant that in the eyes of those newly in charge, he wasn't as well suited for the tasks in the field as they would like.

Dwayne would have loved to adopt Rex as a pet, but the navy donated him to the San Diego County Sheriff's Office, where he is still at work. "It would have been easy to be bitter or selfish," Dwayne said to me. "I still miss Rex, but knowing that he's still working, doing what he was bred to do and wants to do, I have to put his needs ahead of mine."

That statement exemplifies anyone who does service for their country. The pride in Dwayne's voice was obvious when he told me one final story about Rex. "In one of his first patrols, he was with the sheriff on a call," he recounted. "A perpetrator was holed up in an attic. From what I was told, he was a big guy, a former college football player or something. They sent Rex in there and he apprehended the guy. Rex got his bite, something all these dogs just love, and it was good to know that because of him, some officer didn't have to go crawling into what could potentially be a very dangerous situation."

Dwayne is on the verge of retirement. He plans to work as a civilian in dog training. "One of the things I really like about dogs is that they are honest," he said. "They don't ever try to deceive you, really. I laugh about this now, and I'm really very grateful those recruiters told me that I would have an easy time making the SEAL teams. One of the guys out of that office somehow remembered my name and tracked me down a while ago. He told me that of all the guys he showed that video to, of all the guys that he signed up, I was the only one to actually get through BUD/S. Imagine that. I always finish what I start eventually. It would be nice to finish up with Rex, but he's still got plenty of work left to do. And I want him to finish what he started, too."

15

PONCHO IN PURSUIT

Fallujah, Iraq

Poncho, his handler, and the other SOF team members were hunkered down on their recon and surveillance (R&S) operation. After the team had established 360° perimeter security, they took their positions, out of sight of any Iraqis that might pass through. They sat still and scanned the landscape that looked to the men like nothing so much as the surface of the moon. They were near the city of Fallujah, in an area that was considered to have a high potential for IED placement. They were waiting for any sign of enemy action.

A day into the operation, members of the SOF team observed a NATO vehicle on patrol in the area. As the NATO vehicle traveled along, members of the team also detected some movement just beyond a rocky outcropping about 200 yards away from the SOF team's position. They knew that any time a Coalition Forces or NATO vehicle was in motion, it was vulnerable to attack by insurgents. The insurgents' preferred method of attack was to use any of a variety of IEDs, including ones that needed a lookout to press the trigger when the target passed by the hidden explosives.

The movement the team had detected among the rocks was indeed one of those lookouts. Unfortunately the SOF team was not able to prevent him from detonating the IED, which decimated the NATO vehicle. It all happened very quickly, but they did see the insurgent run to a nearby moped, hop aboard, and speed away.

Poncho's handler gave the dog the "Reviere" command, and Poncho lit out after the man and the moped. Even though it was a slow-moving vehicle, the guy had a head start on the dog of several hundred yards and was already out of weapons range due to the angle and elevation of the team's position. Even if they could have gotten a good, clear shot, there was another complicating factor. As fluid as the rules of engagement tended to be, and as much as the team wanted to adhere to them, they were not 100 percent certain that the man on the moped was the same man who deto- nated the IED. Being 99 percent certain wasn't enough to justify shooting him. Without Poncho being with them and on the chase, this would have turned into another case of a bad guy getting away.

Poncho soon ate up the distance between his original position and the fleeing insurgent. Ignoring the moped and focusing solely on the fact that something was moving at a high rate of speed that he was commanded to go get, Poncho dipped down a knoll and out of sight. The team mobilized and did a hasty leapfrog patrol in pursuit of the man, the dog, and the moped. They arrived at the top of the knoll just in time to see Poncho grab the in- surgent by the back of the right calf, clamp on, put on his brakes, and pull the man from the moped, which cartwheeled a couple of times before coming to a stop. The team continued their pursuit while Poncho continued to hold on tightly to the screaming and dazed insurgent. The team rolled up on them and then apprehended and secured their prisoner after Poncho was released from his target. Poncho's first reward of the day was getting to sink his teeth into the thing, in this case the person, he was told to catch. His second reward was a long tug-of-war session with "Dad," his handler.

—◦—

The man Poncho apprehended did have a trigger on him. He was detained, and under questioning he gave up some valuable intelli- gence information. He was also taken out of the conflict for the duration.

Poncho was able to catch the moped thanks to his maturity and athleticism. When he tore off after his target he was moving about 30-plus miles per hour. That was considerably faster than the mo- ped, which was moving at around 18 miles per hour. Short of the team being able to stop the insurgent before the NATO convoy moved through the area and before the IED was detonated, this was the next best possible outcome.

The reality of the situation was that there were miles and miles of desolate roads with the potential for IEDs to be buried at any point along the way. In addition, in the crowded urban areas, there were the added threats of car bombs and sniper activity. It was impossible to always be in the right place at the right time to prevent the worst from happening.

This was early in 2007, when the use of IEDs by insurgents was at its height. During the three months prior to Poncho and his handler arriving in Fallujah, 257 Coalition soldiers had been killed by IEDs. Another 1,485 had been wounded. In many ways, the words "insurgency" and "IED" had become linked together in our minds. Outmanned and outsupplied, the insurgents relied on IEDs as inexpensive but very deadly ways to inflict both physical and mental damage on Coalition Forces.

The insurgents primarily used two methods to detonate their IEDs. The IEDs themselves ranged from antitank rounds and 105 mm artillery shells they'd buried to home-made explosives, often made from ammonium nitrate. One kind of detonator was a pressure plate that was hidden with buried IEDs. The plates were sensitive enough that a human footstep could trigger the explosion. The other kind of detonator is a remote one, like the one the guy used to blow up the NATO patrol. Lookouts with remote detonators hide themselves in high places, where they have a good view of their target area and also a good chance to escape after the job is done. Poncho prevented that last part from happening.

Tensions were obviously high, and the operational tempo was essentially nonstop. As a community, counter-IED operations were of primary importance. Detecting IEDs was only one prong of the attack. Apprehending or neutralizing insurgents, dismantling IED bomb factory networks, and disrupting funding for those explosives-making operations were also a part of the all-encompassing approach to stopping IEDs. So Poncho and the team were not in the strictest sense conducting a routine clearing operation.

The team was made up of the officer in charge and his communications officer; these were two automatic weapons operators bearing M-60 auto machine guns firing 7.62 mm rounds. For extra security and to offer long-range protection for the point man and the handler and dog, two snipers rounded out the team. Unlike the other patrol operations that I've shared with you, these guys were tasked with holing up in a location where they could observe enemy action.

This kind of monitoring operation may sound far less taxing than a sweep covering dozens of miles, and that's true in terms of footsteps walked. On the other hand, for a dog, inactivity—sitting still and quiet so as not to reveal the team's position—is often more exhausting and difficult than walking a long way. These are high-energy dogs, and being asked to sit patiently, especially when geared up and seeing his handler and the other humans action-ready, is not something a dog is accustomed to or likes.

Fortunately, Poncho is one of the more laid-back dogs. He's definitely not a spinner or a big barker when kenneled. His mellow personality and behavior make him ideally suited to this kind of operation, which generally lasts anywhere from thirty-six to forty-eight hours. For some dogs, an assault or raid—they go in, take names, come out—is better suited to their natures. Poncho is certainly capable of doing that type of operation, but he can also do this more measured kind of activity. He certainly proved he can switch, in an instant, from mellow to full throttle.

— ◼ —

An interesting side note to this story: In March 2008 the number of IED incidents declined to 1,175 for the month. This number was down dramatically from a high of 2,612 in February of 2007. Along with that statistic is this one: By January 2008, the success rate of finding and clearing IEDs rose to a high of 69 percent. There are a lot of factors surrounding this positive trend, and I'm convinced that the use of canines in combat is one of them.

16

KWINTO'S NIGHTTIME RAIDS

Logar Province, Afghanistan
(between the cities of Kabul and Pul-i-Alam)

Despite Kwinto's tendency to vocalize quite a bit, he kept silent as he and his handler went out on point. Along with the team behind them, they moved forward swiftly and silently to conduct a nighttime assault on an Afghani compound where, according to recent intelligence reports, the Taliban and its supporters had reestablished themselves. Though there was a quarter moon in the night sky, Kwinto's tawny coat was less reflective than a blacker dog's would have been.

As the patrol infiltrated farther into the compound, Kwinto frantically began to inhale and feather his tail, indicating that he was in odor. His handler stopped the patrol. All fifteen of the men ceased their forward movement. Based on Kwinto's posture and orientation, the handler determined that the hit was directly in front of them, likely in a large culvert that directed the flow of water. Because this was a raid and not a clearing operation, they didn't take the time to immediately substantiate that there was an explosive in that location. Instead, the decision was made to alter their route. No EOD personnel were along, which further justified the decision to simply mark and note the position and reroute.

The rerouting complete and the tactical infiltration to the set point done, Kwinto next led the team to the compound's specified entry point. His handler released him, and Kwinto indicated once again that explosives were present, this time in the stone wall surrounding the compound. Kwinto returned to his handler, and the team moved to a second possible entry point. Kwinto was sent forward again. For the third time in less than an hour, he detected another possible source of explosives. The operators, already hypervigilant, realized that this was a raid that wasn't going to go exactly as planned. Fortunately, they had Kwinto to make sure they didn't make any wrong moves. It was if they were engaged in a high-stakes chess match, and before they committed to a move, Kwinto let them know if they'd made the best choice.

The third entry point was secured, and the team finally moved through the compound. It consisted of roughly a dozen and a half buildings. Besides the pale moon, no other light was present. They moved from building to building, from room to room, slowly and deliberately. An hour, and then another half an hour, passed. With just three buildings remaining, one of the team members detected a faint sound coming from an adjoining room. During these sweeps, Kwinto and his handler were not on point, so a signal was passed down the line to bring Kwinto forward. Once the target area's location had been identified, Kwinto's handler knelt alongside his canine charge, unclipped his leash, and gave Kwinto the search command. As soon as Kwinto came into that odor, he propelled himself into the room where the noise had been detected. An instant later, the sound of gunfire and a nearly inhuman scream broke the silence.

Inside the room, behind a chest-high pile of sandbags, in an excellent defensive position, a lone Taliban fighter was pinned into a corner of the room. Kwinto had the man grasped in his teeth, just below his left armpit. The man's arm was completely immobilized, but he still had managed to fire off a couple of rounds, more out of reflex than from any intent. Kwinto continued to push and grab, and a few moments later the gun clattered to the ground. The man was subdued and taken into custody.

—▪—

After the operation was completed, the EOD did investigate the culvert. Kwinto had been correct. A large IED, one capable of producing an explosion large enough to likely have killed or wounded all fifteen of those SEALs, had been hidden inside it. If it weren't for Kwinto and his handler, the operation would have become more widely known, but it would have unfortunately been for the significant number of casualties incurred.

That was just the first of Kwinto's hits that night. Further investigation revealed that the first entry point where Kwinto detected odor coming into the compound was rigged with a high-order explosive—in this case a pressure-switch artillery round behind a gate in the perimeter wall. Several other IEDs were found within the compound once the EOD team came in, as well as a weapons cache and other explosive compounds. All signs pointed to this heavily armed facility being used as a bomb-making location. That it was put out of commission and that one more prisoner was taken who might provide valuable intelligence was the best-case scenario. It is impossible to accurately measure what acts of violence and terrorism this operation prevented from taking place in the future by shutting this place down.

What is remarkably clear, however, is that Kwinto's ability to detect multiple explosives in a short time span prevented serious casualties from happening to the Navy SEAL team. This raid took place during a period of heightened activity for IED incidents that began in the spring of 2009. As the United States committed more troops to Afghanistan and Iraq throughout the period from May 2009 to May 2010, the number of IED incidents in those two representative months went from 513 to 1,128, according to figures from the Joint Improvised Explosive Device Defeat Organization. August of 2009 was the single worst month for casualties, with 55 killed and 333 injured by IEDs.

Kwinto was relatively young at the time of the raid, only three and a half years old. He's a high-energy dog with an ear-piercing bark an octave or more higher than you'd expect from a dog his size, to the degree that it's something that nearly everyone comments on, comparing him to an enormous linebacker in football with a high-pitched squeak of a voice. When he started out, he was a real handful. Initially, he'd had some trouble, in that he'd go after his handler and our training staff, but eventually he'd gotten over that and proved to be a very capable dog.

In fact, Kwinto has developed a sense of when he's going to be asked to get into the game. Like that football player before kickoff who strides up and down the sideline in nervous anticipation, Kwinto is a pacer. He takes five steps forward, makes a right-hand turn, takes five steps, and then makes another right-hand turn. He repeats as necessary. This is the routine every time his handler brings out Kwinto's tactical vest. That Kwinto does this in the hours before an operation begins is a good sign. Like the other handlers with their dogs, Kwinto's is always on the lookout for any changes in the dog's behavior that might signal some kind of anxiety. As it turned out, Kwinto was mentally good to go the night they raided the Afghani compound.

Before he put the vest on Kwinto, his handler did another kind of check, as he did before and after every mission. Though in the mind and heart of a handler a dog is not a piece of equipment, he does pay the same kind attention to the dog's operational functionality as he would with a weapon or a vehicle. He maintains that functionality, too. Basically, all this means the handler makes sure the dog is physically ready to go.

Kwinto's handler ran his hands along the dog's body, checking for any sign of cysts, knots, open sores, or any other kind of irregularity. He paid particular attention to Kwinto's joints, especially his elbows and shoulders, checking for any signs of wear and tear. A dog's rear legs, especially powerful ones like Kwinto's, put a lot of pressure on the knee. Their quadriceps muscles are especially well developed, but unlike humans, who have fairly well developed calves to establish some kind of muscular balance, from the bottom of the kneecap to the paw, dogs have little muscle. The handler also examined Kwinto's paws, making sure that he didn't have any cracked nails and that all his pads were in good condition. The carpal pads, the ones highest up on the dog's foreleg, are especially important since they rarely make contact with the ground and don't develop the same kind of callous-type hardness as the rest of the pads; they are mostly used when negotiating very steep slopes. Kwinto showed no signs at all of any discomfort.

As they waited that night to begin the raid, Kwinto paced briefly before settling down at his handler's feet. He sat wide-eyed, watching, and waiting. This was, of course, not Kwinto's first time on an operation like this. He had earned some distinction with another SEAL team on a previous deployment. Under similar circumstances, he'd led a nighttime raid when his handler noticed him responding to human odor and released him. Kwinto proceeded to charge through an area of heavy foliage. Two enemy soldiers, who had been secreted in a grape-field trench, began moving toward a position where fifteen other SEAL team members were. They were carrying AK-47s and were likely about to ambush the SEALs. The handler immediately engaged the first armed enemy from a range of approximately 3 feet and then the second from another 10 feet. Both were killed. Throughout that engagement, the handler was in verbal contact with both his dog and his fellow team members. Afterward, a fuller investigation revealed that the Taliban members' weapons were off safety and that the men were carrying two-way radios. Prior to this raid, the SEAL team had already apprehended more than a dozen suspected Taliban members, as they were infiltrating the area via motorcycles. Kwinto and that SEAL team had clearly been very busy.

The members of Kwinto's team probably couldn't add enough thanks to the dog for the role he played in Operation Enduring Freedom in Afghanistan. In my mind, all these men and dogs are heroes; it's just that some of them like tennis balls more than others.

PART IV

GIVING BACK AND
MOVING FORWARD

17

CARLOS AND ARKO AT EASE

I step outside the house and I can immediately feel it—it's like I've taken my clothes directly from the dryer and put them on. Out here, the heat is like a living, breathing thing that envelops you like some kind of constrictor. Somebody once pointed out to me that maybe I chose this spot to set up operations because it reminded me of what it was like when I was downrange. Another person jokingly suggested that maybe one of the side effects of valley fever was a desire to feel like you have a fever all the time. Could be a little of both, but who knows?

I open the door to the kennel and feel instant relief from the blast of cool air. The dogs are all up; some of them just lie there eyeing me, while others do their morning yoga, and a few others sound off though there's been no reveille. It's the usual morning routine of kennel care, and I don't mind a bit. I've got a couple of new prospects that have only been with me for a few weeks, and five dogs in the middle of their training cycle. The two new guys won't be going out this morning, but after they've been fed their kibble, I'll take them out of their crate and do some basic work with them.

One of them, an 80-pound Dutch Shepherd named Nero,

seems to be having some adjustment issues. He's been difficult to crate up, likely because his original owner and trainer hadn't taken the time to establish positive associations with being in there. He may have been forced into his crate a lot of the time after he'd been corrected for doing something wrong. He's a young guy, just over two years old, and he wants nothing more than to be out and about. I put him on a lead, show him one of the two tennis balls I've got with me, and head out onto my property. I don't do anything too vigorous with him; he needs to digest, just get used to me being with him, handling him. At various points when I let him chase after a few balls, I give him a nice cold drink, making sure to interrupt his gulping it down by taking the bowl away, putting it out of reach in the back of the dog trailer, and then returning it to him. He seems to be getting the message that all good things come from me, that I am his friend.

Just as I'm about done with the two green dogs, my friend Wayne, the incredible trainer, shows up. We find a bit of shade and go over the plan for the day, cursing out the meteorologist who forecast the cooling trend that was supposed to have begun two days ago. When it's time to go to work, Wayne and I head over to the kennel. While he loads up the dogs, I wander down to check in on the other two dogs, my pair of retirees. They've been fed and walked to do their business this morning, but when they see me coming toward them, they're both immediately at attention, eager and hopeful.

"Arko. Carlos. Mornin', fellas, but I've got nothing for you yet. Sorry," I tell them.

Given the demands on my business to provide more dogs to the U.S. government and other customers, these two will have to sit it out today. I have no nighttime exercises planned, so they'll get their time outside later this evening. I feel a bit bad about that. They see the other dogs getting geared up, and after years of active duty, they still want to be going at it despite what they've each been through. I'd like to say that they are a part of some master plan that I developed as I was planning my exit strategy from the navy. I knew that I wanted to work with dogs and do the kind of training I'm doing, but the Arko-and-Carlos factor is something that just kind of evolved. In a lot of ways, the additional responsibility that I've taken on of helping retired SOF dogs find good home placements feels a lot less like work and more like some kind of blessing. You know, most of us who "rescue" dogs feel at first like we're doing something to give a dog a better life. In most cases, and this is certainly true in mine, it's the other way around. The dogs give us a better life.

Given all my ties in the SOF canine community, I suppose it made sense that when these two dogs had ended their stints serving I was contacted. I was told that these were two dogs whose temperaments and characters were such that even being placed with their handlers or in any other more traditional "adoption" scenarios wasn't exactly feasible. They were also not going to be suited for placement and continued work in law enforcement or with another agency. The one option they'd have would be to continue to live at their present location, with the other dogs that are a part of the unit they came from. Given how a team's canines work, that would mean they'd be in their familiar place, but because the priority is on operational dogs, they wouldn't get much attention.

That's not to say that their lives would be miserable or that they'd be neglected if they remained at their location. Quite the opposite is true. They'd receive great medical care and adequate food and attention, but they would likely not be able to get the kind of regular exercise and occasional training that they were used to. It's a testament to the regard in which these dogs were held that those in charge wanted something better for them. They believed that I could provide that added bit of care for these two dogs that had both served with distinction. I had to think about it, and originally the question was whether I would personally take charge of the dogs or facilitate them being placed elsewhere, perhaps with other trainers.

This was a head-versus-heart decision, really. I run a business that supplies dogs to people and agencies that need highly skilled canines. To take on the care of two dogs that would do nothing but be a debit on the cash flow wouldn't be the wisest thing to do from an economic standpoint. To be honest, though, I didn't think about it for very long. The SOF community means so much to me, and dogs mean so much to me, that I told them that I would be honored to take Carlos and Arko. I'd also do anything I could to help with any other dogs down the line that needed placement. Even though these dogs were considered to be government property, once they were released to me, I received nothing monetary in return. I don't care about that at all, because as I said earlier, I am one of those people who is determined to give a dog the best life possible.

Yes, MWDs are technically considered to be government "property." They are accounted for in the same way that a piece of equipment is, as a line item on a budget sheet. Broadly speaking, a dog is not a SEAL team member. There is, however, a movement among military and other canine advocates to eliminate the designation of dogs as "property" and to treat them, not in the same manner as humans, but in a manner that better fits with what they do for us and for the country. Certainly progress has been made in this direction. The dogs are treated by the military as counterparts to their handlers. They get medevaced when wounded on the field; they receive rehabilitation for their injuries, and medals and ribbons for their performance and bravery. There are even memorials for those dogs that have been killed in action. An earnest effort is made, to find retirees, like Carlos and Arko, the best life for the rest of their days.

— ‑

Along with the dogs, I received release of liability papers, their medical records, and their service records. I fully understood the need for those release papers. Given the temperament of these dogs, there is the potential for them to bite me or someone else.

The Department of Defense can't be held responsible for that. So these dogs no longer belong to the U.S. government. They are mine.

I was surprised and impressed, however, when I read the dogs' service records and discovered just how honorably these two had served. Having learned their stories, I am proud to have them at my place.

On a raid, Carlos and his handler were the unfortunate victims of an IED that went undetected. In the middle of an intense firefight, they approached an entryway where a bunch of munitions were cached. Enemy combatants hastily detonated the IED, and the resulting explosion severely injured both the handler and the dog and leveled that entryway. The force of the blast collapsed Carlos's lungs and sinuses and threw him several feet, which resulted in his breaking both his back legs and his hips. When the other members of the team rushed up to assist the fallen handler, despite his own serious injuries, Carlos managed to crawl over to his handler and guard him. It took some time for the rest of the team to calm Carlos down. All the dog knew was that his buddy was hurt and he was going to make sure that nobody else did any damage to him. That's the kind of courage and loyalty these dogs so frequently exhibit.

Carlos and his handler were medevaced out of that area of operation, and I'm pleased to say that they both fully recovered. Carlos healed so well that he eventually returned to operation status and was even deployed again before being retired at age seven.

Arko also served in multiple deployments and was injured during one raid. He was sent in to apprehend a bad guy and was shot in the chest at point-blank range. Despite being shot, he got a good bite on the man and didn't come off of it until his handler approached and gave him the command. The enemy was apprehended, and Arko was flown to an FOB where he underwent surgery and recovered fully. He, too, returned to action. Like Carlos, he was retired at the age of seven, and to be honest, when I saw him when he was delivered to me, I was a little surprised that decision had been made. He'd done more than his share of work, but when he came out of that crate, he was all business.

His nostrils flaring, his scorpion tail flagging, his proud, erect gait chewing up yards at a time, Arko is a template for the ideal Malinois in nearly every way. Carlos was much the same, but in the time I've had him, he's slowed just a bit. It's clear that those injuries to his legs, hips, and spine make him uncomfortable when he's been lying still for a while. He's somewhat slower to get up than he used to be.

I notice things like that when I release both him and Arko, but I imagine that almost everyone else would think they are perfectly healthy. When I approach them both, they still have that keen-eyed intelligence that I just admire so much. The drive these dogs have to work and be purposeful never goes away. They may not be protecting a fallen comrade or staying in a bite when seriously wounded, but these dogs still want to work, still want to be of service. It's because of Arko and Carlos, and the other six retirees that I've placed with others, that I created the Warrior Dog Foundation. It's a nonprofit organization that meets a need that I saw wasn't being met anyplace else.

Because these SOF dogs have such specific characteristics and training, the other MWD organizations and foundations that place retired dogs wouldn't be able to meet their needs. Only someone who has experience and expertise working as a trainer of these kinds of dogs can successfully bridge the gap between their active duty and retired lives.

Every time I go out with Arko and Carlos, whether it's for a bit of ball play on my property or on a training exercise with them somewhere in the surrounding area, I'm reminded of the countless lives that these two dogs, the other dogs whose stories I've shared, and the other dogs whose heroism we don't yet know about have saved. As much as I'm committed to providing the best for them in the years they have left, I'm also deeply hopeful that our military will learn from some of what I see as mistakes of the past. It's my hope that we won't dismantle the kinds of programs that the SOF community has built when we exit the battlefield. Maybe we need to create a network of dogs that act as reservists, dogs that serve in one capacity in the civilian world during peacetime but can be called up again at a moment's notice to serve in an operational environment wherever in the world they are needed. That could be one way for us to remain vigilant and prepared.

I know that if asked, Arko and Carlos would serve again to the best of their abilities. There's the old expression about it not being the size of the dog in the fight but the size of the fight in the dog that really matters. Every day for the past few years, I've seen the truth of that on display. These dogs are all heart, different in some ways from the millions of pet dogs in this country, and even more deserving of the care and attention lavished on them. Actually, as far as I'm concerned they can't get enough respect, love, and attention. I've always admired how little dogs ask for in return for all that they do for us. In that way, they are very much like the servicemen and -women in all branches of our military. These dogs are not only our best friends, they embody what's best about us—the courage, loyalty, and heart of true warriors.

MORE ABOUT THE
WARRIOR DOG FOUNDATION

The Warrior Dog Foundation is dedicated to serving the Special Operations community, families, and Special Operations Forces dogs. The foundation helps to transition these dogs from working and living in an operational environment to their "retirement" at our state-of-the-art kennel facility. We care for each individual dog with dignity and grace, including both mental and physical rehabilitation, for the rest of the dog's life. We also strive to educate the public on the importance of K-9s in the combat environment, and showcase the level of sacrifice these dogs give in support of our troops.

As this book goes to press we are working to establish a scholarship fund for the families of handlers who have been wounded or killed in action. In addition, we are developing plans to build a living memorial and museum for Special Operations Forces working dogs to showcase their talents and display the awards they received for their heroism in combat operations in support of our nation's military.

To find out more about the Warrior Dog Foundation, go to: http://warriordogfoundation.org

APPENDIX:
A BRIEF HISTORY OF
CANINES IN COMBAT

In 2003, when I watched that military dog alert the marines to the presence of explosives in a little hut in a rural area of Iraq, the Navy SEALs did not yet have our own dogs assigned to our own teams. We did sometimes work with dogs we "borrowed" from other units, and SEALs had occasionally worked side by side with trained working dogs for decades. It wasn't until 2004 that SEALs began to use dogs specially trained to meet the specific needs of the teams in house. I'm proud to have been associated with the early years of the development of dogs for use with the SEAL teams. The SEAL team dogs are now a part of the long history of warrior dogs.

DOGS IN WAR FROM EARLY TIMES
THROUGH WORLD WAR I

It's likely because dogs have a shared sense of community that they first adapted themselves to living near and then later with humans. Whatever warlike purpose dogs have served, from sentry duty to detection, they have been employed in some capacity for centuries. Since dogs ceased being nomadic and first became domesticated, humans have recognized and exploited the canines' extraordinarily keen sense of smell, sharp eyesight, and razor-sharp hearing. Going as far back as 4000 B.C., there are murals depicting dogs being unleashed on Egypt's enemies.

There is also a rich historical literature highlighting the use of dogs to protect nearly every ancient city-state and numerous rulers and nations that followed throughout the centuries. Attila the Hun, William the Conqueror and succeeding generations of English rulers and leaders, the Spanish conquistadors, the French leader Napoleon, and the German King Frederick the Great are just a few who employed working dogs. Dogs were valued for their finely tuned senses and their ability to be trained and perform jobs. They were appreciated for their loyalty as well.

Some evidence exists that dogs were used as messengers during the U.S. Civil War, but this was mostly the result of an individual soldier bringing his own dog to battle on his own initiative and not because of any kind of sanctioned use. Dogs did serve as mascots, and many of their names are included in honor rolls. Several statues commemorating the Battle of Gettysburg depict dogs that most likely served as mascots.

Some of the most fascinating stories of canines in military history come from World War I. The trenches where much of that war was fought protected men from enemy gunfire and served as places to store munitions and supplies, but they were also a haven for rats. So Jack Russell terriers were sent to roam the trenches, where they used the famous tenacity of terriers to attack and control the rat population.

More important, though, was the work that the so-called Mercy Dogs did during World War I as a part of the Red Cross's efforts in many countries to help the wounded. Because many of the military working dogs we use today can trace their lineage back to Germany and the war dogs of that nation, I was particularly struck by stories of how the dogs in Germany were trained to find the wounded among the battlefield casualties littered across no-man's-land. The Germans referred to these Red Cross canine workers as *Sanitatshunde*, or sanitary dogs. These dogs were trained to go out onto the battlefield with water or alcohol in canteens and packs strapped to their bodies, in order to offer the wounded some small comfort before the men either were rescued or died. The dogs were also trained to go out to the battlefield, often at night, to find the wounded and return with some identifying token such as a cap or helmet. They were trained to identify and remember the location of the wounded and lead a handler to them.

It is estimated that the Germans used nearly thirty thousand dogs during World War I. Most other European nations involved in the conflict also utilized dogs to varying degrees, but the records don't show an exact number of dogs involved, nor the number of casualties among those canine helpers.

As for the United States, when we first entered World War I, which is often referred to as "the war to end all wars," the country's use of dogs in the military was essentially nonexistent. We eventually used dogs trained by the French and British, but a program to train American dogs and supply our troops with them was never implemented. We did, however, supply the French army with four hundred dogs who went on to serve in mountainous areas as draft animals. They helped to haul artillery shells with far greater efficiency than humans, mules, or horses.

During World War I many countries used dogs as messengers. Obviously, in any military campaign, communication between troops on the front lines and their leaders at the rear is crucial. Often, in World War I, more established lines of communication, such as telephones, broke down. Human soldiers often served as messengers, but they proved to be larger and slower targets than dogs, and they also got fatigued more easily. Also, a human soldier was understandably considered a more valuable military asset to capture. As a result, trained dogs went into service, traveling from position to position while wearing specially designed saddlebags or baskets that held both written messages and carrier pigeons.

One French messenger dog, a mixed breed named Satan, was well-known at the time for his heroism and bravery. Satan proved himself to be invaluable in helping to rescue a group of French soldiers trapped by the German army near the town of Verdun in France. In what would later be considered a famous battle of the war, the French soldiers found their encampment encircled by the Germans and their access to supplies and their phone lines cut off. The French were also without carrier pigeons, which they could have used to alert their command to their exact location. The Germans, however, did know where the French soldiers were, and they pounded the location with heavy artillery. They exacted an enormous toil on what came to be called the "Lost Battalion."

It looked like the French soldiers had no hope of surviving, when suddenly Satan entered the battlefield. He approached the French position, wearing a gas mask, and with a carrier pigeon in a basket on each side flapping their wings. Satan was struck twice by German gunfire but, before dying, managed to complete his mission and deliver the two carrier pigeons.

One of those birds went on to successfully carry a message to the French command about the battalion's location. The French quickly responded and silenced the German fusillade.

A German shepherd named Rin Tin Tin was another famous warrior dog of World War I, but one whose story had a decidedly happier ending than Satan's. In fact, Rin Tin Tin went from the bullet-ridden battlefields of Europe to the star-studded world of Hollywood. He was found abandoned in a German trench by a group of American soldiers, one of whom, Lee Duncan, adopted and named him. Duncan brought the dog back to the States, trained him, and got him work in silent films. Rin Tin Tin became an immediate star and appeared in twenty-seven movies. Fictional stories for radio, television, and books were also created about this hero dog. Some of the roles were actually played by the son and grandson of the World War I canine. Rin Tin Tin and his offspring have been credited with the increase at the time in the popularity of the German Shepard as a house pet.

Sargeant Stubby, as he was unofficially called, was a pit bull who served with distinction in World War I after a somewhat less than honorable entry into battle. In late 1917, his owner, an American soldier, smuggled the dog aboard the ship carrying him and other soldiers to Europe and the conflict. Once the dog was discovered, the military commander on board demanded that Stubby be sent back home, but the dog allegedly saluted the officer with his paw and was allowed to stay. Stubby spent nineteen months overseas, where he helped alert soldiers to the presence of enemies and performed other lifesaving tasks. He returned home to a hero's welcome, eventually earning honors from the American Red Cross, the YMCA, and the American Legion. Stubby was presented with a gold medal by General John Joseph "Black Jack" Pershing, the commander of the American Expeditionary Forces, on behalf of the American Humane Society. The pit bull also met three American presidents during his lifetime. People have always loved heroes, even, and perhaps especially, those who have four legs, bark, and wag their tails.

DOGS IN WORLD WAR II: PROGRAMS LAUNCHED AND LESSONS LEARNED

Despite all the stories of heroism on the part of canines in combat during World War I, after the war ended, no branch of the American military created a formal program to train dogs for use on the field of battle. What did exist at this time was an arrangement going back to the early 1900s between the U.S. military and private contractors to drive sled dogs in what was then called the Alaska Territory. The 10th Mountain Division, originally formed at Fort Lewis in Washington State and later relocated to Camp Hale in Colorado, also included dogsled drivers.

The bombing of Pearl Harbor by the Japanese changed a great deal. That surprise attack, coupled with rumors of German spies coming ashore, heightened the need for tremendous vigilance, and this led to dogs taking on expanded roles within the United States as sentries or guard dogs along our coastlines to help protect vital installations and industries. With everyone willing and wanting to contribute to the war effort, dog owners and dog lovers led a campaign to promote the use of dogs in wartime activities.

Several influential members of the canine community, including the director of the American Kennel Club, got together and established Dogs for Defense (DFD) in 1942. It brought together professional and amateur trainers and breeders as well as private individuals who supported the cause of utilizing dogs to a greater extent than ever before in the American military. At first the military was reluctant to let civilians take the lead in establishing any kind of policy. Eventually those barriers were overcome as the need to protect military depots around the country became an extremely high priority. In July of 1942, Secretary of War Henry Stimson issued an order calling for each branch of the military to train dogs to serve a variety of functions beyond sentry duty. These functions included search and rescue, hauling, detection and scouting patrols, and carrying messages. It was up to each branch to decide for itself how many dogs to recruit and how to use them.

Eventually, however, the quartermaster general announced that the United States would need 125,000 dogs for the army, navy, marines, and Coast Guard combined. American citizens had already joined breeders and trainers in "volunteering" their dogs as part of the DFD programs. DFD had been providing dogs for the army's K-9 Corps, while the navy and marines briefly relied on private individuals and other private sources. All four branches, including the navy, eventually turned to the DFD as a source for suitable recruits.

The DFD established regional centers that accepted "donated" dogs. Each dog brought in was considered a "gift" to the military, and there was no promise to return any of them, unless a dog was deemed not suitable for military purposes. In the first two years, the DFD received 40,000 dogs, of which about 18,000 passed initial inspection. Of those, about 10,000 went on to actual duty.

By August of 1942, dogs were patrolling the beaches and coastlines with their Coast Guard handlers. By the end of the first year of the combined efforts of the quartermaster general's office and the DFD, 1,800 handler-dog teams were on the job doing that work, An additional 800 handlers would be fully trained by the end of the war.

The Coast Guard was responsible for spotting trouble and reporting it. The army was in charge of protecting the coastline and turning back any hostile troops. By May of 1944, it became clear that no hostile invasion was forthcoming and that any acts of sabotage were unlikely. The coastline protection program was drawn down, and the dogs in it were transferred to the army.

One of the places that the army used as a training ground for canines was ironically named Cat Island. Just off Gulfport, Mississippi, the island was an ideal environment for training dogs that might eventually be shipped overseas to combat zones. The island was also the site of a failed experiment to train a group of dogs to be offensive weapons—attack dogs. The program was once classified, but in recent years various stories about it have been released.

Apparently, William A. Prestre, a former Swiss army officer who had moved to the United States, sent a proposal to the War Department in 1942 claiming that he could train a group of dogs to attack Japanese soldiers. He believed that the dogs could either kill the enemy soldiers or cause enough of a distraction that American soldiers would easily be able to take control of the enemy's positions. Army Lieutenant Colonel A. R. Nichols, who was in charge of the Cat Island training center, was swayed by Prestre's proposal. He agreed to get the program off the ground but insisted that the training be done in just ninety days.

Prestre proved to be a very demanding and selective taskmaster. Of the four hundred dogs sent to him, he only approved of twelve for further training. That number was further trimmed to nine. In order to train the dogs, Prestre needed humans to act as "live bait." Japanese American soldiers from the 100th Infantry Battalion and the 442nd Regimental Combat Team were also in training on a nearby island at Camp Selby. From among them, twenty-five volunteers were sent to Cat Island. The volunteers engaged in questionable training practices designed to get the dogs to attack them. They wore protective padding to avoid being injured.

After three months of training the dogs, Prestre put on a demonstration to show their capabilities. It was a miserable failure. The dogs either failed to track and find the soldiers without assistance or failed to attack the volunteers with any kind of ferocity when they did locate them. The program was terminated.

Another training program was begun in 1942, this one by the marines, to teach dogs how to serve in jungle patrols in places like Guadalcanal and other islands near the Japanese mainland. These were places where the marines suffered high casualties, as the dense vegetation made them particularly prone to ambush and sniper fire. Again, DFD served as the liaison between dog clubs, private citizens, and the military. The Doberman Pinscher Club of America was particularly involved in this effort, and the marine dogs became known as Devil Dogs. This nickname actually had its origins in World War I; it was a name the Germans gave the human marines they encountered in battle. The first Devil Dogs served in squads of four canines—three scouts and one messenger dog—along with six men. Platoons were comprised of three squads along with an officer, sixty-five men, and eighteen scout and messenger dogs. The first deployments were in the Solomon Islands.

The Marine Corps assigned a rank to the dogs that served, based on their length of service. Each one began as a private first class and advanced to master gunnery sergeant after five years of duty. Dogs could also receive honorable or dishonorable discharges. All of this was put in place in the hope of developing a fighting spirit among the canine corps. At first, the dogs were trained for typical canine sentry duty, but the marines also wanted the dogs to be combat participants, given the nature of the work they did. In early 1943, a scout and messenger dog-training program began.

These early U.S. programs were instrumental in shaping later thinking. The leadership within both the army and marines realized very quickly that civilian trainers who'd worked with dogs in police or private training environments didn't have the background needed to be effective in combat situations. As a result, handlers began to be drawn from the troops. Another lesson learned was that the fourteen weeks the marines spent in training scout and messenger dogs could be too intensive. Without proper rest and relaxation during training, a dog's performance actually got worse instead of better.

The army's Quartermaster Corps prepared 595 dogs for scouting duty to serve in the K-9 Corps. Each of their squads consisted of eight dogs (four scouts and four messengers) with eight handlers. Seven units were attached to a corps or division in Europe and eight in the Pacific. The 42nd War Dog Platoon played a critical role in the Battle of the Bulge and then worked sentry positions at supply depots in Belgium. Other dogs guarded communications lines and led infantry patrols. Similar to what I would experience several decades later, many men serving in World War II reported that once they saw dogs in action as scouts on patrol, they never wanted to go out without canines and handlers again.

Sometimes, though, Mother Nature intervened to keep dogs from showing their true effectiveness. Several officers within the army's chain of command lobbied hard and long for the use of dogs as haulers during the Battle of the Bulge because the wintry conditions made it difficult for men and machines to do the work of moving materials and supplies. More than two hundred dogs were trained and dispatched to France and Belgium, but the needed training time delayed the dogs' arrival. By the time they arrived, the weather had warmed and the snow had melted, which made the dogs less useful than if they had been able to be deployed immediately. This was just one example of how the time frame needed to get dogs effectively trained and deployed had its drawbacks. Another drawback was the relative lack of experience anyone had in training dogs for warfare.

Other shortfalls occurred because during training dogs were exposed only to small-arms fire, but once in theater they were surrounded by artillery fire. While most messenger dogs completed their missions, there are various accounts of dogs being so spooked by the intensity of the sounds of heavy artillery that they didn't make their appointed rounds. In hindsight, it's easy to assign blame for these oversights, but an important point to keep in mind is that the United States didn't have extensive experience in using dogs in combat situations. This became just one potent example of the need to train dogs by creating situations as close to real armed conflict as possible. In addition, the need to expose dogs to every possible environmental stimulus (from noise to light to odors and more) became clear. Fortunately, those of us who came later benefited from these learning experiences.

DOGS IN THE KOREAN WAR AND
THE VIETNAM WAR

At the conclusion of the fighting in World War II, the Quartermaster Corps continued to be responsible for the canine programs. Most of the dogs in the programs were reassigned to sentry duty.

When the Korean War began in 1950, some dogs began to be transferred from sentry duty back to combat duty. The 26th Infantry Scout Dog Platoon, which had been training in Kansas, was immediately deployed to Korea and eventually earned a citation for its outstanding work in hundreds of missions. The citation identified the particular strengths of the dogs working on point, noted that casualty figures would have been greater had they not been there, and gave particular praise to the handlers and others working with them, who earned numerous awards including Silver and Bronze Stars. After the fighting stopped and the peace agreement was signed, many canines were transferred to patrol the newly established demilitarized zone between the two Koreas.

By the time the Vietnam War began, the military realized the various valuable roles dogs could play. MWDs were employed in four main activities during the Vietnam War: scouting, tracking, sentry work, and water detection. Water detection isn't about detecting water. Instead, it's about detecting the presence of human beings in and under the water, with the goal of defending the navy's bases, ships, supplies, and personnel.

During the Vietnam conflict an air force MWD named Nemo served with honor and a degree of heroism that may not have made him a household name like Rin Tin Tin but were remarkable nonetheless. A German shepherd, Nemo was sent to Tan Son Nhut Air Base to work with his handler among the 377th Security Police Squadron. In December of 1966, the base came under enemy attack by the Vietcong. Two handlers released their dogs to pursue the enemy, and the dogs were killed in action. The dogs did not die in vain. They alerted the air force to the presence of the enemy, which enabled the security forces to kill thirteen guerrillas. Later that same night, Nemo and his handler, Bob Throneburg, were on patrol near a cemetery adjacent to the airbase. They took on enemy fire, and both were wounded. Even though Nemo was struck by a bullet that entered his right eye and exited his mouth, he continued to pursue the Vietcong, enabling Throneburg to call in the support of a Quick Reaction Team. Despite his wounds, Nemo crawled back to Throneburg and covered him with his own body. Though they were still under fire and Throneburg sustained a second wound, they were rescued from the field. Both eventually recovered.

Nemo returned to the United States and Lackland Air Base, the site of the air force's dog-training center. He lived there as a mascot and recruiter for the program and made personal and televised appearances. His presence at the training center served as a reminder of the importance of the relationship between a canine and his handler.

While the vast majority of dogs that served in Vietnam were German shepherds, Labrador retrievers served with distinction on Combat Tracker Teams (CTTs). CTTs had two main purposes: to make contact with the enemy and to detect recent enemy activity in the area. The CTT units faced the same issues we do today with our SEAL team dogs and handlers. They train separately for a while and then the SEAL MWDs and handlers have to integrate themselves into the larger force. The overall easygoing ways of Labs made this relatively easy, and their keen sense of smell and innate tracking skills, sharpened by training, made the men quickly change from thinking *What is that dog doing here?* to *Why didn't we always have these dogs?*

In addition to their tracking work, the CTT team dogs were used to locate lost and missing friendlies. Together with a larger force working in advance of the CTT troops, the program was a success. However, the contributions of the CTT Labrador retrievers and their handlers didn't receive a great deal of publicity or acclaim. In fact, the program was phased out entirely in 1970, but it has never been forgotten by breed enthusiasts and some of its participants and supporters.

Labrador retrievers also worked with the army as part of tracker teams. The difference between a scout team and tracker team is this: Scouts search an area for signs of an enemy's presence; trackers do the same but also then pursue that enemy aggressively. In all, nearly a dozen army tracker teams worked in support of U.S. troops during the Vietnam War. In addition to pursuing human targets, MWDs in Vietnam searched for explosives, as our dogs do today. That detection work was complicated by the fact that the Vietcong frequently used caves and tunnels, but the dogs' adaptability to foreign environments and their courage and other attributes allowed them to rise to the challenges and get the work done.

Estimates vary, but as many as five thousand dogs and ten thousand handlers served our country from 1964 to 1975. The sad reality is, with a few exceptions like Nemo, those dogs did not return to the U.S. The reality of warfare resulted in handlers having to either set their dogs loose to fend for themselves or turn them over to the South Vietnamese Army. Either way, it had to be a horrifically painful decision to leave a valued teammate behind.

DOGS IN A POST-9/11 WORLD

It seemed as if, after the Vietnam War ended and peacetime resumed, once again little real thought was given to how much dogs
had aided us during the conflict. Training dogs to be combat-ready
stopped, and dogs that had participated in the war were reassigned
to sentry work. Unfortunately, it would take an attack on American soil to get the military to pay attention to the need for dogs
to be part of an ongoing, active defense of our country and military personnel. September 11, 2001, served as a wake-up call and
a rallying cry in many ways.

On that day, my fellow SEALs and I quickly realized that the
course of our service lives was going to change. I can't say that
other teams besides Team Six wouldn't have begun to use canines
if it weren't for 9/11, but certainly that horrible event triggered a
need for heightened security on the civilian side and hastened our
preparations for the eventual conflicts our military engaged in.

In New York City, one of the attack sites, dogs played a promi-
nent role in returning the lives of the citizens to "normal." Interest-
ingly, since 2001, there has been a 17 percent decline in the number
of New York City's uniformed police officers, while the number
of canine cops has doubled. Today, 100 dogs are on the force in
New York, working in the narcotics, bomb, emergency-response,
or transit squads. Working dogs are a familiar sight even to those
of us who don't live in major metropolitan areas.

The Department of Defense has spent nearly $20 million on
explosive detection since 2006. Noncanine detection units have
had a 50 percent success rate, but the canine units raise that number by another 30 percentage points. That's a huge increase, and it
is little wonder, then, that the Navy's Special Warfare brass came
to the same conclusion as New York City and other agencies—dogs
are the best detection "tool" available.

GLOSSARY

A School   advanced, on the job training in the Navy

AK   a kind of assault rifle; one of the most popular is the AK-47

Boatswain   a noncommissioned officer on a ship in charge of the maintenance of the vessel, its boats, and other equipment

BUD/S   Basic Underwater Demolition/SEAL, the navy SEAL training program

C-4   a common kind of explosive

Carrier pigeon   a pigeon that carries messages; carrier pigeons were especially used to get messages to and from troops in the battlefield during World Wars I and II

Clearing operation   a military operation designed to clear an area of all enemy personnel, mines, or other obstacles

Cobra Gold   annual training exercises conducted by the U.S. military in Thailand between U.S. armed forces and Asia-Pacific military personnel

Corpsman   an enlisted member of a military medical unit

Demilitarized zone   an area from which all soldiers and weapons have been removed after an agreement to stop fighting is in place

Downrange   a combat zone

EOD   Explosive Ordnance Disposal; EOD members remove and dismantle IEDs and other explosives

Esquive   French for "dodge or sidestep"

Firebase   an area in a war zone where artillery can be housed to provide heavy firepower

FOB   forward operating base; a secured military position for U.S. troops fighting in another country

Force Reconnaissance   a special operations force of the U.S. Marine Corps

Fusillade   shots fired at the same time or in rapid succession

Green Berets   a special operations force of the U.S. Army

Guerrilla   a member of an unofficial military unit, often fighting to overthrow a government

High-value target   most often a person, but sometimes a thing, that is important to the completion of an enemy's mission and that an opposing force tries to capture; as an example, Osama bin Laden of the militant group al Qaeda was an extremely high-value target who was eventually captured and killed by U.S. Navy SEAL Team Six

Humvee   a High Mobility Multipurpose Wheeled Vehicle, or a four-wheel-drive military automobile

ICOM radio   two-way radio communication device

IED   Improvised explosive device, a kind of homemade explosive

In country   in foreign territory, especially a combat zone

In theater   in military terms, a place where the action is

Insurgent   a person who revolts against established authority or government

JDAM   Joint Direct Attack Munition, a kind of guided bomb

Klick   a kilometer, which is about two-thirds of a mile (.62 mile) or about 3,200 feet

Maritime   related to the sea

MARSOF   a special operations force of the U.S. Marine Corps

Multipurpose K-9   a trained working dog with more than one skill set; Navy SEAL dogs, for example, are often trained to detect explosives and also apprehend "bad guys"

Munitions   military supplies, such as weapons and ammunition

MWD   military working dog

No-man's-land   unoccupied land that is under dispute

On comms   communicating with headphones

Outpost   troops stationed away from a forward operating base

Paramilitary   a military-like force that isn't officially a part of any country's military

PKM   a Russian-made machine gun

Quartermaster general   staff officer in charge of supplies

Rack   military term for bed or cot

Rangers   a special operations force of the U.S. Army

RDX   Research Department Explosive, an element found in many military explosives

Reconnaissance   exploring and gathering information behind enemy lines

Seabee   a member of one of the construction battalions of the Civil Engineer Corps of the U.S. Navy

SEALs   the U.S. Navy's elite special operations force; SEAL stands for Sea, Air, and Land, the ways they are able to literally approach a mission

Security perimeter   a boundary where security controls are in place

Shalwar kameez   traditional clothing worn by some Afghanis

SOP   Standard Operating Procedure

Sympathetic detonations   detonations usually caused unintentionally by a larger nearby denotation or explosion

The War to End All Wars   term used for World War I

Trench warfare   a kind of fighting used in earlier wars that involved troops fighting from the protection of trenches or ditches in the ground

COMMANDS USED WITH MWDs (FROM THE DUTCH)

Braaf   a word of praise

Los   "Release!"

Reviere   "Search for a person!" (used in apprehension work)

Szook   "Search!" (used in detection work)

REFERENCES

Air Force Special Operations Command. "Heritage of the Combat Search and Rescue Professionals." http://www.afsoc.af.mil/library/afsocheritage/afsoccsarheritage.asp.

Alabama A&M and Auburn Universities. "The Dog's Sense of Smell," June 2011. http://www.aces.edu/pubs/docs/U/UNP-0066/UNP-0066.pdf.

Alsop, Nigel. *Cry Havoc.* Chatswood, NSW, Australia: New Holland Publishers, 2012.

Bilger, Burkhard. "Beware of the Dogs." *The New Yorker,* February 27, 2012.

Cawthorne, Nigel. *Canine Commandos: The Heroism, Devotion, and Sacrifice of Dogs in War.* Berkeley, CA: Ulysses Press, 2012.

Congressional Research Service. "U.S. Military Casualty Statistics: Operation New Dawn, Operation Iraqi Freedom, and Operation Enduring Freedom." September 28, 2010.

Cordesman, Anthony H., Marissa Allison, Vivek Kocharlakota, Jason Lemieux, and Charles Loi. "Afghan and Iraqi Metrics and the IED Threat." Center for Strategic & International Studies, November 10, 2010. http://csis.org/publication/afghan-and-iraqi-metrics-and-ied-threat-afghanistan.

Elson, William Harris, and Christine M. Keck. *Junior High School Literature*. Glenview, IL: Scott, Foresman, 1920.

Johnston, J. M. "Canine Detection Capabilities: Operational Implications of Recent R & D Findings." Institue for Biological Detection Systems, Auburn University. June 1999. http://www.barksar.org /K-9_Detection_Capabilities.pdf.

Lemish, Michael. *War Dogs*. Dulles, VA: Potomac Books, 1999.

Merritt, Sue Rogers. "Combat Tracker Teams: Dodging an Elusive Enemy." *Vietnam*, October 2001; http://www.historynet.com/combat -tracker-teams-dodging-an-elusive-enemy.htm

Nosaka, Ray. "Secret Mission: Dog Training." *The Hawai'i Nisei Story*. http://nisei.hawaii.edu/object/io_1153256967265.html.

Pets for Patriots. "America's Four-legged Warriors." http://m.military .com/off-duty/pet-corner/2012/05/07/military-working-dog-americas-four-legged-warrior.html.